# BRAVE NEW CHURCH

# Brave New Church

## WHAT THE FUTURE HOLDS

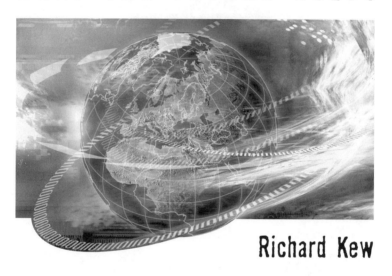

Richard Kew

MOREHOUSE PUBLISHING

**Morehouse Publishing**
P.O. Box 1321
Harrisburg, PA 17015

*Morehouse Publishing is a division of The Morehouse Group.*

Design by Corey Kent

**Library of Congress Cataloging-in-Publication Data**

Kew, Richard, 1945–
    Brave new church : what the future holds / Richard Kew.
        p.    c.m.
    Includes bibliographical references.
    ISBN 0-8192-1870-7 (alk. paper)
1. Episcopal Church. 2. Anglican Communion—United States—
Forecasting. I. Title.

BX5933 .K475 2001
283'.01'12—dc21

                                                              0049631

Printed in the United States of America

01  02  03  04  05  06  07  08  09    10  9  8  7  6  5  4  3  2  1

I dedicate this book to
the next generation of young Christian leaders,
especially my son-in-law and elder daughter,
Joseph P. Fickus, III, and Olivia Kew-Fickus,
as they train at seminary for ministry in tomorrow's world.

\* \* \*

10.13

103014

10/30/14

# CONTENTS

# FOREWORD

Having co-authored several books with Richard Kew over the last ten years, it is now my pleasure to commend this, his latest product. Relying on a tried-and-true methodology, Richard Kew follows our shared tradition of identifying the trends that form a foundation for attaining a greater depth of knowledge of the church's journey in today's world. This appealing process invites the reader to identify those signposts that can direct and shape strategies, focusing our discipleship. Such "markers" enable us to understand and interpret the landscape that we are about to pass during this time of change and transformation. It is an approach that has proven to be most fruitful and, surprisingly to both of us, frequently accurate.

In the last book we wrote together, *Toward 2015—A Church Odyssey*, we lifted up what we anticipated would be the necessary ingredients for the church to be more focused on "the main thing"—that which Christ calls us to be as Church. To be those who proclaim the Gospel and invite those who do not know Christ to "come and see Jesus." To be a part of a church that spends much of its time and energy on forming committed disciples and not just producing nominal members. This enables all of us to live out our faith and to become servants of the Servant, Jesus Christ, who is always one for others.

The trends identified in *Toward 2015* were utilized by the Episcopal Diocese of Texas, for example. They took the ingredients, distilling them as they developed their own clear vision for a fast-moving, fast-growing future. This Texas approach to being a mission-driven people is, in turn, being used by as many as half the dioceses of the Episcopal Church as they have begun to interpret and implement their own vision in a variety of ways.

When looking at the Episcopal Church or any other main line Protestant church, an objective observer would see a church moving in various directions. One part would be enthusiastically implementing this clear vision, while others are attempting to deal with ideological differences in very different ways; some would believe that a strict biblical interpretation of God's will would lead to isolation or would propel them to leave the fold. They would discover, however, that for those of us who are Anglicans in our present polity, there are few places to go.

Yet another part of the communion would push the envelope on moral and social issues, seeing in them the way to live out God's will. Frustrated in this enterprise, they would end up impatiently acting on their own before the whole body decides to act.

Such an observer would conclude that those who are devoured by the internal ideological issues within the Body of Christ, in fact, hinder the mission of the Church. For Anglicans, God's will is revealed in scripture and discovered as we live out of our faith in daily life. Truth is revealed when God's will is revealed in both life and in scripture and brought together into a new direction. What is so distressing is the failure to implement the mission of evangelization, formation, and ministry and service while we dig in our heels believing we are the bearers of the truth!

By utilizing the trends identified by Richard Kew, we all can come to a better understanding of the territory into which we are called to further Christ's kingdom in the midst of our culture.

Although not a new concept, the two elements that comprise a clear vision in the midst of rapid change remain constant: the hope of the Gospel (what we ought to be), and a significant understanding of a particular mission context (what is). Failure to address this predicament leaves us aimlessly wandering with little foundation for our actions.

Identifying the impact of trends ranging from globalization and crumbling old denominational hierarchies to developing young vocations and thousands of newly planted congregations, calls us to prayer and to serious theological work. With such insights, not only can we build a foundation, but we can also find a clear direction and, in turn, find the opportunity to proclaim Christ in our culture.

The lesson of this book is that "to be forewarned is to be forearmed." That is precisely what trend identification can be—an opportunity for us to forearm ourselves for what might be around the corner.

The Church, by participating in God's mission, is called to advance into the rapidly changing world of technological and cultural changes-that Christ may be made known and God's children may be given the opportunity to respond to the Gospel proclamation.

May we all be better equipped for mission by the "markers" of this work. May the landscape become more user friendly, so that we may engage the Gospel of Jesus Christ in God's good creation, which is ever-changing, forever revealing newness of life in and through our sisters and brothers and in all the vastness of God's creation.

Roger J. White
Bishop of the Episcopal Church
Diocese of Milwaukee

# INTRODUCTION
# Trends Come . . . And Trends Go

*The practice of dividing the world up into a list of mega-trends might at first seem a little arbitrary. Its purpose, how-ever, is not to render life simplistic or superficial, but to establish a categorical foundation on which a greater depth of knowledge can be built.*[1]
John Naisbitt and Patricia Aburdene,
writers and trends analysts

### Shenandoah Inspiration

In the summer of 1989, our family was traveling back home to Tennessee along Interstate 81, through the wonderfully beautiful Shenandoah Valley in Virginia. When my wife was ready to give me a break and take her turn behind the wheel, I made myself as comfortable as possible in the passenger seat, and began doodling—literally on the back of an old envelope. By the time we reached Roanoke, I had the beginnings of a list of trends I was able to identify that were shaping the life of the church. In another couple of hours, by the time we reached the Virginia-Tennessee state line, I realized I was onto something.

Although all this happened only eleven years ago, comparing the world as it was then with how it is now, it seems more like eleven generations! The 1990s turned out to be an incredible era of change and transformation.

On that sticky summer day the Berlin Wall had yet to fall, and Saddam Hussein was still considered a friend by the U.S.A.—albeit a rather unstable one. The elder George Bush was president of the United States,

Margaret Thatcher was the prime minister of the United Kingdom, and Mikhail Gorbachev was in the process of bringing glasnost and perestroika to the then unreconstructed Soviet Union. How much happened during the last decade of the Second Millennium!

Those doodles on the back of that envelope were eventually destined to become a book—the first that I wrote with my good friend Bishop Roger White of the Episcopal Diocese of Milwaukee: *New Millennium, New Church.*[2] Bishop White, unbeknown to me, had been making his own set of similar observations at that time. As I look back at that little book, I realize that like almost everyone else's attempts to track trends, we got some things surprisingly right, and other things entertainingly wrong. In the forecasting game no one bats a thousand. This can be seen by the performance of meteorological sages of the Weather Channel, sports pundits, hardened gamblers in Las Vegas, and Wall Street gurus.

Speaking of Wall Streeters, I am sure that most of them would have scorned anyone who suggested that as the millennial year 2000 dawned, the Dow Jones Average would be five times what it was in 1989 at over 11,000 points. Only two years earlier the stock market had taken that incredible nosedive, the federal government's deficit was ballooning out of control, and the American economy was not at all sure where it was going. What a difference a decade can make.

### Trends Revisited

As we begin to get used to living in a brand-new millennium and century, following a decade of the most colossal changes, I have once again fallen prey to the temptation to trend-track. On that August day in 1989, as I started trying to define the trends, it was for an audience of one—myself. Traveling around the church and the country as the director of a mission agency for four years by that time had given me a unique and panoramic perspective on what was happening around the church and around the world.

The exercise with the old envelope was my looking for some way to give order to what I was seeing in my travels, which then led to the impulse to attempt to assess how all this might pan out in the long-term. Bishop White and I joined forces when we realized that we were both thinking and exploring in similar directions, despite sometimes significantly different presuppositions. Since then I have been regularly published on the topic of trends and the future to a growing audience in and beyond the United States; and I realize that when I put something into writing now, I need to exercise a little more care than we did in those cavalier earlier days!

Throughout the 1990s, I continued to travel far and wide throughout North America and beyond. All through my wanderings, I have instinctively sought to understand what is going on, how realities are changing, and how this relates to the trends that I began teasing out on that long car drive through the glorious Blue Ridge Mountains and the lush Virginia countryside. What follows is the outcome of the several years that I have spent reviewing the positions we took a decade or so ago, measuring them against the present realities, and attempting to posit what the future might hold in store.

John Naisbitt, who popularized trends analysis with his 1980s book, *Megatrends*, reckons that once a trend is in place it might peter out in six or seven years, although it could have a much longer life. The reason for this is that the culture today turns over so rapidly that what might have been normative five years ago is by now outdated and gone. While some of the trends that we documented a decade ago are still strong and healthy, others are losing (or have lost) their momentum.[3] More important, the world and the church continue to change at an astonishing pace, which requires a constant refocusing of our perceptions.

This present book is intended to be a short catalogue of some of the new concerns that look as if they will (or should) confront us during the years ahead. To appreciate the significance of these trends, a reader does not need to agree with every aspect of the worldview that I am presenting, but I hope my ideas will stimulate people to, perhaps, craft their own set of trends to provide something of a framework for their own work and ministry.

### The Difference between Prophecy and Forecasting

Let me repeat at the outset what I have said so often in the past, both in the spoken word and in writing: Like the Old Testament figure, Amos, many generations ago, I do not claim to be either a prophet or the son of a prophet (Amos 7:14). Based on the observations made and the information that has been accumulating over the years, I am attempting to envision the shape of the challenges that are ahead of us.

I am, as it were, charting some of the concerns that look as if they are going to shape our lives and ministries during the next ten to twenty years so that as they impinge upon our work they do not take us totally by surprise. As was the case with my previous books and articles, there are times when I have taken a leap of imagination, reaching the conclusion that seems to the casual reader that two and two could very well add up to five. Please bear with me, but invariably there is more information that has shaped my conclusion than space will allow in a book like this. In light of the evidence that is before us, the developments that are spelled out in the following pages warrant our attention, since they may profoundly affect our lives for the foreseeable future—perhaps as far ahead as 2020.

We watch the weather forecast before going out on a picnic or for a day spent walking trails in the mountains, so that we will be dressed and equipped for as many of the climatic variables as possible. None of us expects the forecaster will ever get it 100 percent right, but most of the time they give us a pretty good idea of what we should do or take to keep ourselves warm, cool, dry, or all three! So it is with the trends that I will be outlining.

Several years ago William A. Sheridan, a Boston-based consultant and strategic planner, wrote a book pooh-poohing the idea of prediction. The opening dozen pages of his book do a sharp and cynical demolition job on our capacity to foresee what might be coming down the pike. Were it not for his tone, much of what he said was too close to the target for someone who enjoys teasing out such trends—yes, we do get things wrong. Nevertheless, having wielded his wrecking ball pretty successfully he then turns 'round and writes:

> However, just because we cannot predict it does not mean we can ignore the future. We must continue to plan for the future by considering scenarios of what might happen and adapting our plans accordingly. To do otherwise would be foolhardy. We cannot blind ourselves to all predictions, because some contain vital information about our environment—not necessarily what *will* happen but what *could* happen.[4]

You don't need to be a rocket scientist to uncover most of the trends that I have highlighted in this book. Some are there before your very eyes, jumping up and down, shouting at the tops of their voices, and drawing attention to themselves. Others require a little more ferreting around; but nonetheless, they are part and parcel of our environment and will influence the way we live and the way we minister in the years to come.

Both in the world and in the church, the last ten years have been far more traumatic than ever I imagined on that summer day in 1989 when I jotted down my thoughts on the back of an old envelope. I had begun my trend-watching several years after I had been drawn into the serious study of the future, and this predated the world-changing events that took place around 1989, symbolized by the fall of the Berlin Wall. At that time we were still coming to terms with the revolutionary impact of the fax machine upon our ability to communicate with one another, while relatively few people were listening to the hype that surrounded an idea that some were quaintly calling the "information superhighway."

At that time existence in most of the denominations may have seemed pretty fractious, but despite that, church life certainly was much kinder and gentler than it was to be during the final decade of the twentieth century. All this has meant that certain ideas, issues, and circumstances that looked as if they would play a fundamental role in the life of the older, mainline denominations either have not emerged or have run their course more rapidly than anticipated. In the midst of such rapid and groundbreaking change, it is hardly surprising that a whole bevy of new forces has elbowed its way to the center of the stage.

While there is a whole array of trends worth tracking, what follows are the top ten candidates that I believe we will need to take into account as we journey into this new century, and the third millennium of the Christian era. Consider each one carefully, and ask how it is likely to impact your own life, your parish, and your involvement with the wider church as it seeks to undertake its mission, beginning on the doorstep of your own home, and even to the ends of the earth. Accompanying each chapter are questions and resources that will help you explore more fully some of the issues and ideas that have been raised. If you wish to continue the conversation that *Brave New Church* has started, then come along to my Web Site, *www.TheKewFiles.Net*, where there are more opportunities—bulletin board and chat rooms—to follow through on what you find in this book. This book as been designed to stimulate debate, which leads to informed action, rather than to present authoritative answers to all of tomorrow's challenges.

Once you have grasped what these trends are all about and how they might have an impact on the work of God in your neighborhood, then it is vital that you use them creatively to develop your own strategic response, replete with long-, medium-, and short-term goals and objectives. It would be an excellent idea to gather together a group to work on this with you. Talk, argue, and pray over the broader circumstances within which you are ministering, being both as thoughtful and as constructively critical as possible.[5]

Despite the fact that this era is an unsettling one in which to live, it is also one of the most exciting since the apostolic age to be a Christian. Looking at the emerging world, it would appear that God is giving us the kinds of opportunities for which our forebears would have given their right arms—it is up to us whether we build upon these advantages or botch things up entirely.

Christians have been called to faithfulness. Consequently, we must grasp the opportunities that God thrusts in our direction, and use them wholeheartedly on behalf of the Eternal One whom we serve, and the Son, Jesus, who has redeemed us. This book is intended to help us perceive the array of opportunities that are at hand.

# TREND ONE
# Globalization Will Continue Apace

*Globalization ... is a complex drama, with the final act still not written. That is why under the globalization system you will find both clashes of civilization and the homogenization of civilizations, both environmental disasters and amazing environmental rescues, both the triumph of liberal, free-market capitalism and a backlash against it, both the durability of nation states and the rise of enormously powerful nonstate actors.[1]*
Thomas L. Friedman, *New York Times* columnist

### The Arrival of the Global Village

This isn't the first time in human history that massive globalization has taken place, but it is clearly the most extensive. The first event that played a part in globalizing the world was expansion of the Roman Empire, the world into which Jesus Christ was born. The comparisons between the Roman world and our own are fascinating—a common language, relative ease of communication, and ready interaction between cultures. Grasping this reality should help us to understand the New Testament world better.[2]

However, the whole modern process of globalization began around 1840 when sail began to give way to steam; the increasing omnipresence of a British Empire that exercised a world-encompassing trading policy was the catalyst. Two world wars and the Great Depression (1914–1945) temporarily reversed the process of globalization, but since the middle of the last century it has progressed relentlessly, its ad-

vance fueled during the 1990s by the political, social, cultural, and economic fluidity that accompanied the end of the Cold War, coupled
with rapidly improving communications.[3]

It is going to take a crisis of cataclysmic proportions to bring to an
end the rapid process of planetary integration that quickened to break-
neck speed as we swept through the last ten to fifteen years. Such a
calamity could, of course, happen, but to demolish thoroughly the
sometimes carefully and sometimes carelessly constructed unifying
process that has been going on will require a convergence of crises of
gargantuan proportions.

Several leading candidates could precipitate such catastrophe, one
being a total economic meltdown. This could be caused by a massive
shift of international investment away from the United States, the re-
assertion of tariffs and barriers to international trade, or a political
backlash coming from the nations and groups who figure they are the
losers in the helter-skelter dash to benefit from globalization. While the
advantages do tend to outweigh debits, "globalization is a savage
process," and not everyone is happy at what is happening.[4]

Other possibilities are the devastating consequences of a pandemic
or other international health crisis, a major ecological disaster, or either
a world war or a regional conflict that reverberates outward into other
geopolitical arenas. If any or all these calamities were to occur—and
given the speed of communication and the fragility of our ecosystem
they cannot be ruled out—then virtually all the trends that I am going
to be outlining in the following chapters would be up for grabs. Should
this happen, we would more likely be dealing with issues fundamental
to human survival.

My bookshelves groan under the weight of a wide selection of the
doom-and-gloom scenarios painted by various authors who have
made a good living from their writing throughout the years. While such
books sometimes sell well, most of these doomsday scenarios have either spluttered or come to naught. However, the time surely may come
when someone reads the signs of the times correctly and, as a result,
hits the disaster scenario jackpot. This, of course, depends on the convergence of numerous unpredictable variables.

At present, I find myself watching several global hot spots and sets
of indicators, which, if a whole series of misfortunes were to occur all at
once, could trigger chaos.[5] An English analyst, who was recently forced
to resign from the RAF because of his views, has of late posited the distinct possibility of all-out global hostility around 2006, with China as a
key player in that war. Certainly, East Asia and the China Sea is a region

fraught with frailties, as is China's long and meandering border with Russia along what the Chinese call the Black Dragon River, and the Russians the Amur.[6]

But it may not be armed conflict that triggers a spiral downward into some kind of global crisis. Certain economists are deeply concerned about the levels of debt being carried by the world's two largest economic powers—Japan and the United States of America. While the Japanese have loaded themselves up with public sector borrowing in an effort to kick start their ailing economy, "America's public prudence has gone hand-in-hand with private profligacy" that showed little sign of abating in the foreseeable future.[7] For example, in December 1999, Americans far outspent their earnings—thus increasing household debt levels significantly. Similarly, the volatility of stock markets, the interdependence of national economies, and the fluctuation of currencies, can all send ominous economic shock waves around the world.

Any or all of the above possibilities, writers William Strauss and Neil Howe would assert, are setting our society up for a great "Unraveling." Coauthors of several influential books on generational theory, notably *Generations: A History of America's Future, 1584 to 2069*, and *The Fourth Turning*, Strauss and Howe suggest that if their assessment of the cycle of generations and history is correct, then it is almost inevitable that a major catastrophe is brewing. Furthermore they predict that it will tumble in upon us during the first decade of the new century—and its impact will ricochet around the world for years to follow.[8] Writing in 1996, they said:

> In the middle of the Oh-Ohs, America will be a very different society than in the late 1920s, when the last Crisis catalyzed. The nation will be more affluent, enjoy better health, possess more technology, encompass a larger and more diverse population, and command more powerful weapons—but the same could be said about every other Unraveling era society compared to its predecessor . . .
>
> A spark will ignite a new mood. Today, the same spark would flame briefly but then extinguish . . . This time, though, it will catalyze a Crisis. In retrospect, the spark might seem as ominous as a financial crash, as ordinary as a national election, or as trivial as a Tea Party. It could be a rapid succession of small events in which the ominous, the ordinary, and the trivial are commingled . . . At home and abroad, these events will reflect the tearing of the civic fabric at points of extreme vulnerability.[9]

Given the stability of the post–Cold War world, it is prudent to listen carefully to Strauss and Howe's warnings, but it is important that
we entertain a healthy suspicion of the inflexible and deterministic
straightjacket into which they thrust events and history. While there are
various potential clouds on the horizon that could prompt the Unraveling that they perceive as inevitable, at the moment there are no full-
blown storms in sight.

It is true that one should never portray such clouds as entirely be-
nign, and that each has the potential to set in motion a torrential storm,
but while each chapter of history might be shaped by certain similar
waves and patterns, it does not predictably repeat itself. Yet there will always be lots of wild cards out there that could quickly alter the situation, heralding significant changes.

We saw how rapidly things could happen when the Persian Gulf
Crisis burst in upon the tranquility of August 1990. I was leading our
congregation's Vacation Bible School the day the Iraqi leader, Saddam
Hussein, invaded the small neighboring country of Kuwait. Like almost
everyone else, I was taken by surprise, not having kept my eyes on this
latest episode in the interminable squabbles that were going on in the
Middle East, so this foolhardy military action came like a bolt from the
blue of the summer sky. Perhaps the moral of such events is that it is
wise to keep a weather eye open for what might be going on.

### A New Global Generation

As the electronic communications revolution has integrated the world,
kids are able to keep in closer touch with one another. The ideas, values,
and tastes of those who are now in their twenties downward are shaped
less than previous generations by the various cultures in which they
have been raised, and more by a seamless media network that increasingly blankets the whole world. "Thanks to the Internet, satellite news,
porous national borders, and the end of the Cold War, they are also becoming the world's first generation to grow up thinking itself as
global."[10] Whether they live in the outback of Australia or the high Hi-
malayas, a cohort of kids is rapidly growing to maturity whose whole
approach to life has more in common with other members of their own
generation almost everywhere else in the world than with their elders,
their parents, their neighbors, and their own ethnic groups. They tend
to wear the same clothes, listen to the same music, and flock to the same
movies, with the result that little by little their worldviews are being integrated, overriding many (but not all) of their cultural distinctives.

While it is true that billions of members of the rising generation are so poor and downtrodden that they do not have access to all the artifacts of this global culture, the very fact that this globalizing culture exists influences them and their values. A South African friend of mine writes, "It is not simply *access* to these things (i.e., the Internet, MTV) that counts, but the effect that their very existence is having on the youth, even if they only *know* about it and don't have it at home."[11]

I stayed in the guest house of a respected central African university some years ago on the night the senior class graduated. Having lived on or near several American and British college campuses during most of the last thirty years, I can vouch that the loud parties going on all over the campus were just as noisy and were accompanied by just the same music, fashions, and fads as you would find at universities in the West. In the few years since then, MTV and other purveyors of these components of Western culture have been advancing aggressively, and due to satellite technology, such programming can now be picked up in more than 160 countries. Meanwhile, CNN and, to a lesser extent, BBC World television are busy interpreting events to everyone everywhere. Add to that the culturally unifying power of the Internet, and you have a forceful mixture of converging influences.

But let me hasten to add that the culture of these rising younger generations is not as predominantly American as people seem to think. What is emerging is a distinctly mix-and-match approach to life, facilitated by the media and accelerated by the Internet. While the young do cling onto many components of their cultural origins, they are more prone than their elders to mix in a little bit of whatever strikes their fancy from wherever it might have originated in the world. While children might gain great pleasure from the Pokemon fad that had its roots in Japan, their elder brothers and sisters will be listening to groups that come from France or Sweden, while their young adult cousins are eating at Ethiopian restaurants before going off to watch movies that were made in Africa for American film companies, and directed by Italians!

John Micklethwait and Adrian Wooldridge are a pair of economic journalists who have worked hard to grasp the impact and progress of globalization. They have concluded that while a lot of "globaloney" is talked, behind the statistics a different way of looking at things is emerging. They point out that those under thirty are much more likely to automatically think in world terms. They are almost nonchalant about the way they pick up the phone to make international calls, for example, and they expect products and ideas to be instantaneously available all over the world—whether we are talking about older men being able to get their hands on Viagra, or children being able to read the next installment of the adventures of Harry Potter.[12]

It remains to be seen how the consciousness of this rising generation of young men and women will give shape and structure to the way humans relate around the world as they mature—and take the reins of control from those of us who are much more the product of a preglobal age. It is likely that they will not see national and ethnic differences in quite the same way as those of us who are older do. There may be great blessings in store because of their greater tolerance of diversity, but hidden within it there could also be unforeseen (and unforeseeable) difficulties.

One facet of the globalizing culture is unprecedented migrations of millions of people all over our planet. As families follow work and opportunity, or flee from tyranny, they take their children and young people with them, further blending and internationalizing the youth culture. This means that American elementary schoolchildren in Middle Tennessee not only hear about the fate of their peers being sold into slavery in Sudan from the media, but learn firsthand what it means from their Sudanese classmates. Meanwhile the administrators of that same school district, which only a few years ago was culturally virtually monochrome, are now wrestling with the challenge of educating children who speak several dozen different languages and began their lives on five different continents.

Meanwhile, college students from all over the world are flocking to North America to gain valuable experience and learn American English, while the number of young Americans going abroad for study continues to double with each passing decade. "An increasing number of (American) students are looking beyond such predictable destinations as Britain, France, and Spain to Eastern Europe, Latin America, Africa, and the Far East. In 1996, fourteen countries each attracted more than one thousand American students. Such people return to, say, Michigan convinced that their first novel, though set in Ann Arbor, should be a meditation on a Hindu incantation."[13]

We can be certain that in the long-term this plethora of global influences that is shaping the young will continue to profoundly affect the way they are formed and how they handle themselves. In the years to come we will see it profoundly influencing the way they behave, think, dress, do business, establish families, believe, entertain themselves, and so forth. All this will inevitably shape the lives of those who have made some kind of Christian commitment, and will impact on the churches to which they belong as we move further into the new millennium. At the moment, most local congregations seem almost oblivious to this potential revolution taking place under their very noses.

### The Global Village

Meanwhile, despite the sometimes violent attempts of protesters to disrupt the World Trade Organization meeting in Seattle in December 1999 and other global economic gatherings, telecommunications and liberalized trade seem likely to continue creating the global village of which Marshall McLuhan dreamed in the 1960s. In such a world, everyone is functioning in a global playing field. Even when goods and services are primarily intended for domestic markets, the standards that businesses and organizations work to, as well as the competitors they fear the most, are inevitably going to be global ones. To launch a small one-person business today, especially if its marketing strategy includes the Internet, means to launch into a planetized marketplace.

Experts are divided over whether this is good, bad, or merely a neutral thing. Certainly, the global consciousness that is emerging is what various people have called a McWorld consciousness. The common elements of this consciousness are that it is highly materialistic, generic, and thoroughly secularized—and secularizing. Christian leaders from the Global South, like the Anglican Archbishop of Nigeria, are just beginning to voice their concern about the way McWorld ideas are being soaked up by youngsters in their lands. This has led some of them to wonder whether their churches will be able to retain the loyalty of the next generation as they face such an onslaught.

This new culture is putting incredible pressures upon people, their families, and their working lives, fed as it is by a spirit of greed and acquisitiveness. Even as the world is being drawn closer together, we are seeing the stresses and strains of fragmentation tearing individuals, communities, and their households apart. Not only does the McWorld approach to economic development have the power to tear at the fabric of family life and communal structures, but the marketplace's sometimes ruthless exploitative dynamic accelerates the degradation of the planet's environment and all our ecosystems.

These are all factors of which those of us in the churches need to be acutely conscious as we develop our mission strategies. Local congregations seem to think of themselves as too small to have much influence in such a world, but the reality is that they are the Christian frontline. Tom Sine, America's leading Christian futurist, expresses the challenge before us in this way, "McWorld is driven by the aspirations and values

of modernity and is aggressively at work creating a one-world con-
sumer culture in which the shopping mall is replacing the church as the
center of religious devotion, and all of life is reduced to a commodity."[14]

As mass communications, urbanization, and changing patterns of
commerce reshape the world, making the global village ever more real,
a whole variety of internal, psychological, and intellectual factors will
continue to radically alter the way both young and old alike think.
Christians cannot continue to bury their heads in the sand over the implications of such a massive sea change going on, and because of the
global nature of our faith we are probably among those best equipped
to face up to its challenges effectively and creatively.

### Globalized Denominations

Globalization is, of course, having a profound impact upon the communal life of the various families of churches. In the Anglican Communion—the international fellowship of Christians of which the
Episcopal Church is the primary American "franchisee"—the pressures of globalization were felt when bishops gathered in 1998 in Canterbury, England, as they do every ten years at the invitation of the
Archbishop of Canterbury to confer and consult with one another.
This most recent Lambeth Conference of Bishops, as it is known, illustrated how the Anglican approach to being Christian is in the process
of graduating from a loose coalition of local provinces to a global
church, with a global consciousness. This will alter structures significantly in the coming years.

We have for centuries affirmed whenever we recite the Nicene Creed
that we "believe in one holy catholic and apostolic church," but in truth
we have had little grasp of what it means to be part of a universal and
international Christian body. The effect of globalization is that we must
now learn how to live in harmony with one another despite our diver-
sities. The reality is that whether we are Anglicans, Lutherans,
Methodists, or Roman Catholics, to name but a few of the various
Christian traditions, it takes a lot of patience, diplomacy, and tolerance
to hold together such a varied and competitive network of power players and ideas. This in turn then puts enormous strains upon a church's
local fabric.

The various traditions are wrestling in their own way with many of
the same concerns. For example, a distinct pan-Evangelicalism has
emerged, with its own inner tensions and challenges, while many of the
same issues are being pushed to the top of the agendas of other de-

nominational families. However, despite the fact that most Protestant groupings that span the world are united by their commitment to the authority of the Holy Scriptures, they do seem to lack the historic cohesion and, therefore, interdependence that goes hand-in-hand with being a church that honors some kind of historic succession.

Globalization entirely alters the structural balance—we become "glocal" people, as some put it. At the same time that pan-national frameworks are asserting themselves, pressure is coming upon the structures from the opposite direction, and we are watching local congregations claim more and more autonomy and independence. Decisions made by each local unit of believers are becoming more important, even if they are wildly at odds with what might have been Christian tradition and practice to that point. The effects of this independence then ricochets, profoundly impacting the larger whole: not just that local unit's own national structure, but even the whole Christian community around the world. The battles over human sexuality are a prime illustration of this.

Telecommunications now means that we all live in each other's backyards, and we are discovering as a result that we need to develop sensitivities to each other's culture, ethnicity, theology, and our various shortcomings. It seems only yesterday that we were praising the ability of the fax machine to overcome the uncertainties of mail services, enabling us to keep in closer touch with one another. The fax has now become a boring and old-fashioned communications technology over which we tend to yawn. Today we have e-mail, and the expanding capacity of the Internet is already stretching to inexpensive voice mail, audio-, and video-conferencing from everywhere to everywhere—and in a very few years these things will be normative.

What is going to have the most profound impact upon those of us who are Anglicans is the rapid advance of connectedness in Africa. Wired phone systems have been fraught with problems in Africa, but the various satellite communication networks are beginning to zero in on that huge market, so that cellular communications are rapidly leapfrogging traditional telephone systems. As this happens, more and more African Anglicans will inevitably become involved in the international discussion, determined that the rest of us hear their voices and listen to their concerns. This is a reality that illustrates how ecclesiastical circumstances are intricately bound up with economic, political, ethnic, and technological facts that govern life universally.

For several years now I have moderated an online conversation about mission, ministry, and the future.[15] What began as a handful of

American Episcopalians and Canadian Anglicans chatting about the issues confronting us, quickly became a large group of forward-thinking Christians from all over the planet. As I write these words, members of the *Toward 2015* conversation can be found from the Arctic Circle in the north to the balmier climes of Latin America. Filipinos raise questions that Irishmen attempt to answer, and insights from Singapore, New Zealand, South Africa, and other lands are routinely shared. All this is very healthy, because it challenges the prevailing perceptions of North Americans, who until now have lived a somewhat parochial existence.

The listserv technology we use is hardly state-of-the-art by the rapidly developing standards of online life. But such a forum would have been utterly impossible—or impossibly expensive—until just a few years ago, and totally beyond the reach of all but the most well-heeled and sophisticated international corporate bodies. Yet the conversation, which is sent around the world from a modest server in the back office of a missionary society in Ambridge, Pennsylvania, continues day after day, dealing with topics too numerous to count.

All this means that none of us can act in our own backyard as if it is not going to have an influence on the church elsewhere in the world. Just as the scandals of Christians killing Christians in the tribal pogroms of Rwanda in the mid-nineties reverberated around the world, so are events and controversies in the U.S.A. or Scotland heard now around the world. Nigerian colleagues have told me how difficult it can sometimes be made for Christians in some of their congregations, when the hullabaloo about sexuality, for example, roils the waters of the churches in the West, and is then reported in their local newspapers. Muslim detractors take great glee in pointing up these items or lifting news off the Internet that tells of some leading Western theologian or cleric calling into question the fundamentals of Christian belief.

Certain ecologists have this theory that when a butterfly flaps its wings on one side of the world, it can profoundly influence weather patterns on the other. Similarly, today's ease of travel and the communications network that now connects every corner of this planet mean that not only can we eavesdrop on one another's deliberations and conversations, but we can often involve ourselves in what is going on elsewhere. We have to think and act locally, while realizing that there is no artificial line of demarcation that shuts off the local from the global—which means that from hereon out we *must* accept the reality that the church is always going to be a global people.

### The Global Mission Endeavor

Global mission is also becoming an omnidirectional enterprise. During the first two-thirds of the twentieth century most missionary activity was from the developed world to the developing, from the global north to the Global South. Personnel, resources, and money flowed out of the rich West, even when it was struggling with the effects of the Great Depression and world wars, to every corner of the planet where missionaries had been permitted to penetrate.

Yet the final third of the last century saw this whole missionary enterprise that was once dominated by Westerners turned on its head. The churches that had been planted by this great missionary movement not only started to undertake cross-cultural missionary work of their own, but they are now in the process of moving into the lead in the business of global mission. As the nineties advanced and the millennium came and went, a trickle of missionaries from the younger churches has turned into a veritable flood, the number of missionaries sent from nonwestern countries overtaking the number sent out by churches in the West.

Not only are representatives of these churches concerned to re-evangelize the West, desiring to work with us as we seek to turn the tides that have flowed so strongly against Christianity for so long, but they are setting out to an array of destinations all over the world. For example, Graeme Codrington, my South African friend, writes, "Many of the people who go to the 'West' from the Global South go with real missions in mind, and *do* missions as well. In fact, many South Africans are in the forefront of helping American organizations to adapt their middle-class program to fit into inner-city, multicultural environments."[16]

While traveling around the world, I have met Korean missionaries in Argentina and Russia, Africans who are working in the West, and Latin Americans who are serving in Europe. Meanwhile, Christians from India have scattered all over their own vast subcontinent, and China is experiencing the most significant Christian growth. Since the earliest times, the Christian faith has been a religion with legs, and as it has become the pre-eminent global faith, so followers of Jesus have started going with the Good News from everywhere to everywhere. This is happening again, but this time with a different cast of characters.

Even with the ending of the Cold War, there are countries, regions, and ethnic groups that are beyond the reach of traditional missionary

methods, yet the 1990s saw new and creative approaches being pioneered, many making use of the Internet—particularly the rise of the
"nonresidential missionary." If the Roman roads accelerated the spread
of the gospel during the first and second centuries, so the great information superhighways of our age are being used by mission agencies
like Anglican Frontier Missions to enable networks of Christians to
support the founding and development of congregations in places
where Christianity is either alien or forbidden.[17]

But there is a significant amount more to mission than that. It
would have been impossible and unthinkable for leaders actively to involve themselves in the affairs of churches, not their own, on the other
side of the world just a few years ago, but now this is part of the daily reality. In addition, until recently, centralized mission boards were almost
a necessity if congregations were to have meaningful relationships
overseas. Now, many of the services they once rendered are increasingly
redundant.

Congregations are now finding great joy as they develop links with
congregations in other parts of the world with little help from ecclesiastical intermediaries. A number of relationships between Orthodox
parishes in Russia and Episcopal congregations in the U.S.A. took root
during the 1990s. Once introductions had been made, and parishes had
been helped over their initial awkwardness with each other, many have
gotten on together as if they had been friends for a lifetime—despite
horrible language difficulties and divergent cultural perceptions and
conditioning.

Furthermore, ease in travel means that teams of Christians are increasingly fanning out across the globe to involve themselves in short-
term projects. There are any number of churches in the developed
world that are sending groups of adults and young people to participate
in everything from building schools and churches to undertaking
Christian education in the Caribbean, Latin America, and beyond. One
of the fastest growing areas of ministry for the Episcopal Church's
largest voluntary missionary agency, the South American Missionary
Society, is its work with short-term mission teams.

Short-term mission projects are some of the best ways that those in
the West can be introduced to the *real* rather than *tourist* world beyond
our borders—and learn some significant lessons about both life and
the missionary challenge. Meanwhile, folks from "over there" are coming to our countries bringing blessings with them, and in the process
making deep and lasting friendships in Christ. The flow of resources
and ideas going in both directions can be considerable.

### Death to the Tyranny of Geography

What we saw happening as the twentieth century closed was a taming of the tyranny of distance. This shrinking of the planet looks certain to continue into the foreseeable future. As exciting as this increased measure of connectivity appears to be on one level, it is probably going to take a long time for us to know how to make this new reality really work in our favor. We are likely to make a lot of mistakes, and coming to terms with a world with porous boundaries will be high on the agenda of the church during the early years of the new millennium. One Roman Catholic leader says that these new situations "tend to promote tension between the openness toward others and emphasis on one's own identity, both of which are beneficial attitudes if the right balance is maintained between them."[18]

The adjustments necessary will require us to take a crash course in what it means to be part of a global family. This brings us back to the Nicene Creed, and our affirmation of faith "in one holy catholic and apostolic church," alluded to earlier in this chapter. Now we are being challenged as individuals, parishes, and national churches to live out what we say we believe. This all-encompassing globalization of world society and culture will lead us in a lot of unexpected directions, as churches, nations, and ethnic/cultural groupings.

This means that Christians in the West can no longer either act or make major decisions in isolation from the global family of believers—and, in a different kind of way, how we relate to those who belong to different religious traditions. The truth is that for a long time our actions and decisions have had global implications, but we have either been unaware of them, or have only remembered this when it has been to our advantage. The global village has now fully emerged, and there is an interconnectedness that far transcends nation, tribe, race, or tongue. From our local churches to our national networks we are now enmeshed in a thickening web of relationships—and whereas thousands of miles and radically different cultures once provided more than adequate insulation from one another, those relationships now require a level of accountability with which we are unfamiliar.

Thus, it is hardly surprising that Christians living as a minority religion in the midst of a hostile culture are deeply distressed by some of the ethical and theological experimentation that is going on in some of the churches of the West, as they struggle to come to terms with being God's people in a culture that has shed most of its Christian heritage.

Neither is it surprising, on the other hand, that Western Christians puzzle over some of the idiosyncrasies of churches only recently planted in what had once been animistic societies. Andrew Walls is a Scot, now in his seventies, whose long life has been both full and fascinating. After graduate studies in theology at Oxford, he was sent to teach church history in a seminary in Sierra Leone. He said of his work, "I shared the conventional wisdom of the 1950s about church history teaching; that church history was full of lessons to be imparted to the 'younger churches' from the accumulated wisdom of the older ones."[19] As he set about his work in West Africa, going through that awkward process of adjusting to his new setting, he became conscious of how different this environment was from the one with which he was familiar back in Europe. He then says, "I still remember the force with which one day the realization struck me that I, while happily pontificating on that patchwork quilt of diverse fragments that constitutes second-century Christian literature, was actually living in a second-century church. The life, worship, and understanding of a community in its second century of Christian allegiance was going on around me."[20] In the global village, such insights will come home not only to those who have the privilege of being part of a younger church, but also will be increasingly available to those of us whom the global village has enabled to now peer in on the lives of other Christians elsewhere.

Being part of the universal Christian community, the church has ceased to be an interesting intellectual topic that fascinates only the theologians among us. Before our eyes the affirmation we make whenever we use the creeds has been turned from a relative abstraction into a practical reality that makes a challenging new set of demands upon us— as well as providing some fascinating and world-altering opportunities.

## *Disintegration*

One final observation about the growth of globalization is needed at this point. In the last fifteen to twenty years we have watched the framework provided by old-style industrialization disintegrating, and a whole new wealth-creating infrastructure—whose reach is instantly global—taking its place. This commercial transition has at times been painful, but it appears to be an inevitable and necessary accompaniment to this major chapter change in human history. The same thing is now happening in the life of the church, and there is good reason to believe it will not be comfortable in the ecclesiastical arena either. Inevitably in the next few years we will be forced to jettison structures and approaches that might hinder our ability to undertake the mission to which we have been called by our Lord and Master. In their place new and startlingly different structures and approaches are bound to emerge.

When we wrote *New Millennium, New Church* at the beginning of the nineties, Bishop Roger White and I foresaw that hierarchical structures and centralized bodies would give way to networks. This has been happening, although vested interests and a timid conservatism have maintained yesterday's hierarchies far longer than they deserve. Nevertheless, what was important in the past is now largely irrelevant, absorbing precious resources and often diverting rather than enabling the church's primary task.

These outdated approaches to organization are now not only luxuries we do not need, but ones we can no longer afford, although they will not disappear without a struggle. I suspect an array of experiments in organization will pop up, some ill considered—even foolhardy—while others, once planted and given a chance to shake out the bugs, will bear fruit thirty-, sixty-, a hundredfold. A generation from now we will probably look back and wonder why we put up with yesterday's ways for so long. However, we may also be amazed that the way in which we organize ourselves for mission will have changed.

I suppose the message to us as we enter the twenty-first century, the first truly global era, is "Hold onto your hats, my friends, it is likely to be a bumpy ride—but you can bet it will be exciting!"

+ + +

### To Think and Talk Over

1.  How have you found globalization impinging on your personal life and the life of the community in which you live?
2.  How do you think your community would fare if there is the kind of Unraveling that William Strauss and Neil Howe talk about in their books, and is summarized in this chapter?
3.  Look at the lives of the first global generation and those of older people, and figure out the different forces that have shaped them.
4.  What advice would you give to a leader of the African, Asian, or Latin American churches about how to deal with the influence of modern secular life upon young people?
5.  What are the advantages and the shortcomings of the development of global denominational families?
6.  Is geographic distance a tyranny, or is it a necessary buffer keeping people of different religions, cultures, and ethnic groups apart?

7.  What do American and European Christians have to learn from
    their African, Asian, and Latin American counterparts? Are we will-
    ing to listen to them?
8.  Think about what it means to be part of "one holy catholic and
    apostolic church," and consider some of the practical implications
    for the twenty-first century.

### Suggestions for Further Reading

Barber, Benjamin J. *Jihad vs. McWorld* (New York: Random House,
    1995).
Friedman, Thomas L. *The Lexus and the Olive Tree* (New York: Farrar,
    Straus, & Giroux, 1999).
Huntington, Samuel D. *The Clash of Civilizations and the Remaking of
    World Order* (New York: Simon and Schuster, 1996).
Kaplan, Robert D. *The Ends of the Earth* (New York: Random House,
    1996).
Kaplan, Robert D. *The Empire Wilderness* (New York: Random House,
    1999).
Sine, Tom. *Mustard Seed Versus McWorld* (Grand Rapids, MI: Baker
    Book House, 1999).

The following are two very useful periodicals:
*Foreign Affairs*—The bimonthly journal dealing with international
    issues.
*The Economist*—The global news weekly of global affairs, politics, com-
    merce, culture, science, and technology. *The Economist* also has an
    excellent Web edition that can be reached at www.economist.com.

### Web Sites

*A Word about Browsers:* While everyone has a favorite Web browser, I
have found the www.NorthernLight.com browser to be an excellent
tool for searching in particular areas on the Internet, and for research-
ing this book. Northern Light puts the materials it identifies into fold-
ers and subfolders, enabling you to search more specifically. This means
that if you ask a question about "Thomas Cranmer," for example, you
will receive the various items the browser identifies, and it will also
break them out into topics. You can look at the subfolder entitled "Anglicanism" to get a better understanding of the resources available on
the Net to learn more about the great archbishop's relationship to the

founding and development of Anglican Christianity as a distinct Reformed and Catholic tradition in the worldwide church.

- *The Global Center, Samford University*
  *www.samford.edu/groups/global/about.html.* The Global Center at Samford University, Birmingham, Alabama, is one of the best-equipped Christian settings dealing with the whole issue of globalization and the global challenge. It has a well-maintained list of links with sites dealing with global statistics, refugees, population, etc.
- *Global Mapping International*
  *www.gmi.org.* The purpose of Global Mapping International is to provide maps and other resources to enable us to understand the world better for the purpose of effective mission. This Web Site has a selection of links dealing with the whole issue of mapping and statistical analysis of the world.

# TREND TWO
# A Process of Radical Ecclesiastical Reconfiguration

*Both the church and the world are always in flux, but usu-*
*ally we bring to that constant change a stable and unchang-*
*ing paradigm, a mind-set that sometimes lasts for centuries.*
*Sooner or later, however, the thousands of minute shifts and*
*changes bring such pressure to bear that the stable mind-set*
*cracks, shifts, or falls apart. That has happened to us.*[1]

Loren B. Mead, Episcopal priest and visionary

### Tectonic Changes on the Church Scene

Whatever your presuppositions and perspective, there is the steady ac-
cumulation of evidence that we are at the starting line of a major ecclesiastical reconfiguration. Globalization, which is affecting every other
human endeavor, as we saw in the previous chapter, is now playing an
increasingly important part in the way the church remakes itself. It
seems inevitable that the ecclesiastical arrangements that have prevailed for several centuries, and with which we have become quite comfortable, are now coming to an end. Churches are spilling beyond the
national boundaries that once contained them, for example, while
within those borders "the old denominational hierarchies are crumbling, and the dividing lines between the various communions within
Protestantism are blurring."[2]

Richard Foster, writer and founder of the spirituality network Ren-
ovare, wrote to his supporters at the end of 1999, "We are at the tail end
of a major form of Christian expression, an expression we have known
for nearly half a millennium . . . Denominational loyalties no longer de-

18

fine the religious landscape. The people of God did quite well long before the rise of denominations and they will do quite well after they have gone."[3]

While what follows focuses upon the Anglican/Episcopal facets of North American church life, many of the observations being made are equally relevant to most other denominational traditions, also. George W. Bullard, Jr., is a thoughtful pastoral coach and observer of the mainline denominational scene. He writes, "Denominations that continue to focus the legislative aspects of their corporate life on highly decisive social and political issues will find that they make great contributions to splintering of denominational families. In a trend within this trend, increasingly younger generations of Christians will find their way into congregations that meet their spiritual needs for faith, focus, and family. Often these congregations will be either the more conservative congregations within their own denominational family, congregations in more evangelical denominations other than their own, or quasi-denominational or nondenominational congregations."[4]

In addition, while North America has a variety of distinct national and regional personalities, which should not be ignored or underestimated, there are so many commonalities between Canadians and those in the U.S.A., that these days I increasingly find myself thinking of English-speaking America more as a single whole than as separate and distinct units. All this is part of the global convergence that is taking place, particularly in the older developed countries, and which is reflected in the lives of the various denominations. While there are still significant local distinctives, we all face many of the same challenges and are tending to deal with them similarly.

Despite these convergencies, this splintering is taking place and accelerating. Political groups adhering to theologies deeply at variance with each other are tearing at the fabric of the church, the tensions being focused by such hot-button issues as radically differing perspectives on human sexuality. There are deep tensions over this issue within each of the old-line denominations, with breakaways, particularly among conservative Christians, being threatened against Methodists and Presbyterians, for example. Meanwhile, in the Episcopal Church, a number of congregations have already split away from traditional geographical dioceses to become part of Anglican communities overseas, rather than remain under the charge of the bishop in whose jurisdiction they are situated—and with whom they find themselves at odds.[5]

Yet the first signs of radical change pale beside the consecration in January 2000 of two American Episcopal priests as bishops to serve as "missionary bishops" in the geographical region where the Episcopal Church has until now been the primary franchisee.[6] The two men, John H. Rodgers, Jr., a retired seminary dean, and Charles H. Murphy, III, a parish priest from South Carolina, following their consecrations in the cathedral in Singapore, became bishops of the Anglican churches in Southeast Asia and Rwanda respectively. They were then sent back to the U.S.A. to provide oversight and missionary leadership to biblical and orthodox Episcopalians who found themselves at odds with the prevailing structures.

Since that time they have been gathering dissident congregations that want to remain part of the Anglican Communion, but do not wish to belong to the Episcopal Church any longer, working under the title the Anglican Mission in America (AMiA). At first, they lay low as the church digested what was happening, but as the year 2000 progressed, it was clear that a very different approach to organization was going to be tried. Anglican Mission congregations still consider themselves part of the worldwide Anglican Communion, but belong to units of that Communion that are rooted and grounded in other parts of the world—Southeast Asia and Rwanda.

Not only does this development point to the lack of trust that a significant proportion of bishops worldwide have in the direction in which mainline American Anglicanism is going, but the long-term implications of this event are extraordinary. This new approach challenges the primacy of geographically ordered dioceses and judicatories, and, perhaps, will initiate a whole series of experiments with different approaches to organization. People are now seeking to relate by affinity, not locality. What makes it different than previous divisions is that large portions of the Communion have not dismissed the initiative out of hand. Being deeply critical of what they consider to be the compromised theological and ethical stance of the ongoing mainline church, portions of the Communion are cooperating and encouraging such experimentation.

Following the General Convention of the Episcopal Church in 2000, Bishop Murphy rallied his troops.

> I am writing to tell you of some tremendously encouraging news that, perhaps, you have already now heard—"We have a liftoff!" Just as the ground crew rejoices when a shuttle is successfully launched by NASA, we can now rejoice that the groundwork you have worked with us for nearly three years to lay has launched the Anglican Mission in America . . . We are

no longer an interim action aimed only at extending pastoral care to embattled congregations within the Episcopal Church of the U.S.A., but, rather now, an Anglican missionary movement, under the oversight of two Archbishops and their two Provinces (Rwanda and S.E. Asia), aimed at creating a new, orthodox Province that is fully connected to the larger Anglican Communion through the Provinces that are overseeing this work.[7]

Then in August 2000, there was a series of meetings in Nassau, Bahamas, at which the Episcopal Church came under scrutiny. Further seeds were planted at those meetings that could result in the development of a full-blown "confessing" movement within the Episcopal Church. Significantly, at those meetings steps were made toward the recognition by conservatives remaining in the mainline church of the consecrations of Rodgers and Murphy.

If all this sounds confused and messy, that is because it is! It is likely to stay that way for the foreseeable future. As one friend, a relatively new bishop, has said to me, "I suspect that we will have to learn to live with organizational ambiguities for the next fifteen or twenty years, as this whole thing works itself out." I would suggest that whatever Anglicans or Christians in other traditions do in the months and years ahead, *all* the ecclesiastical structures with which we are living at the moment should be seen as temporary and interim as we explore our way toward something more appropriate for changing times.

Then there is the network of deepening ecumenical relationships that Anglicans are forging with people like Lutherans, with whom they are entering into ever-deeper filial relationships.[8] The convergence between these traditions will inevitably further reshape the way the American church undertakes its mission, and with it will come a whole other set of pressures. Add to this the huge variety of official and unofficial networks of large churches, small churches, Generation X congregations, and so forth that are emerging everywhere, and it is possible to see something new being born.

Rectors of large and theologically conservative Episcopal congregations have told me on many occasions that they have much more in common with peers outside the Episcopal Church serving congregations that are of a similar size to their own, and with whom they meet regularly, than with most of the smaller congregations of the diocese in which they might be situated. The question is whether they would ever act on these commonalities, forging even more substantial ties—and in the process loosen ties with the dioceses of which they are formally a part.

Denominations unaccustomed to the radical new reality that is emerging, with its strong global overtones, tend to default back to tried-and-true responses, rather than being willing to experiment with organizational innovation and nontraditional alignments. Anglicans, for example, continue to look down with some suspicion on those who do not share their commitment to bishops in the historic succession, while all of the old-line churches have preferred to cozy up only with those who belong to, or are sympathetic with, the National Council of Churches.

We see something of this determined effort at ecclesiastical line drawing in the comments I received from a Generation X pastor who works in New England. A clergyperson who divides her time between a parish and a nearby college campus congregation wrote me the following: "Both areas where I've served parishes have two separate clergy associations (for mainline churches and evangelicals). The mainline response to 'why can't we have one clergy association?' tends to be 'Aha! you're not one of us! Go join the evangelicals!'—a response that is totally absurd in a post-Christian culture."

A further complicating factor for North American Anglicans is that there is a range of Anglicans who, for reasons both good and bad, at the moment function outside the framework of the historical Episcopal Church of the U.S.A. Certain limitations are placed upon those ordained in the Episcopal Church, to whose discipline all its clergy must submit; however these men and women are sisters and brothers in Christ and, up against an ever more hostile culture, we should surely want to work with them as closely as possible. Other great ecclesial traditions are also wrestling with smaller, and more focused, denominations that share the same perspectives.

Many Episcopalians, myself included, greatly respect the Reformed Episcopal Church, which came into being in the 1870s, as well as many others who belong to those more recent offshoots of the 1970s and 1980s. One of the most delightful pieces of Anglican ecumenicity in North America is the Benedictine Abbey within the Episcopal Diocese of Quincy, Illinois, where Christians who owe allegiance to several Anglican traditions happily share in ministry and mission together.

In the face of widespread challenges to the relevance of the church in the twenty-first century, I hope that in the next decade we will learn to let go of the more selective ecumenism that has marred our grasp of what it is to be part of the whole Body of Christ. Our age is one of fragmentation and atomization, and I am beginning to think that one of the key components of our witness is the ability of Christians to love and work with one another, despite a history of differences.

Jesus spoke a great deal more about being one with one another than most of us are prepared to accept, so influenced are we by our me-first culture. It is all very well to stand firm against compromising truth, but we should not forget that in the mind of our Savior, Jesus Christ, there seems to have been an integral link between truth, unity, and Christian love. The industrial era was one that saw the increased fragmentation of the church as Christians asserted their intellectual distinctives; perhaps the postindustrial age will be one during which we should be encouraging creative approaches to convergence.

### Following in the Steps of Martin Luther

However, what is driving denominational reconfiguration is not so much our relationships with cousin churches, rather it is a whole series of deep tensions that are agonizing all the churches in North America and far beyond. Just as any of the pilgrims entering the abbey church in Wittenberg on All Saints' Day 1517 could not have foreseen the consequences for Western Christendom of the theses that had been nailed to the door by a young Augustinian friar with irritable bowels, so we can only guess the long-term consequences of the tearing, agonizing, arguing, reconciling, politicizing, theologizing, and spiritual anxieties that pervade the life of our ecclesial structures today. William Willimon, writing as if from Jesus talking to the old mainline churches, says, "The best thing about you is your past."[9]

I am convinced that emerging Postmodernity, the untidy bundle of prevailing worldviews that has come on so strongly during the last few years, is in its own totally disorganized manner kicking out from beneath churches of every tradition and flavor a large number of the theological and social props from the past upon which we have leaned for so long. These have supported and shaped what has evolved into today's ecclesiastical configuration over a series of generations. Whether liberal, conservative, or not-sure-of-my-alignment, these philosophical and intellectual structures have given form for so long to the arena in which we have lived out our faith that it is hardly surprising that their decline (and imminent departure from the stage) is causing pain and distress. As they disappear it should also come as no surprise that the denominations and coalitions that have given order to church life have begun to totter—or at the very least, look for new ways to express themselves.

The structures we have received, and which were molded into the present shape by the evolution of the old industrial Enlightenment world, have for the most part backed themselves into a cul-de-sac. Not surprisingly, they are now having terrible trouble finding a way out. Looking at the realities, whether Anglican or from other traditions, there seems to be little or no hope for received church structures if they insist on being tied to their present form. Just as great corporations of the last century, like AT&T and IBM, have had to rework themselves radically to be functional in a very different kind of commercial world, so, too, churches must be prepared to offer up a huge number of their sacred cows from the past, while not sacrificing the substance and content of the Christian message.

The tragedy is that a stubborn spirit of denial *still* prevails among those who purport to be the movers and shakers of most denominations. For many churches today the mood is one of maintenance and survival, not mission and advance. Huge numbers of our ecclesiastical institutions seem totally unable or unwilling to accept the reality of what is going on and are refusing to face up to the flood of changing circumstances that is shaping their world.

United Methodist academic and leader Len Sweet writes, "Unprepared institutions in 'persistent make-believe' can tread water only so long before going under. We have a lot of drowning victims out there, churches a couple of funerals away from closing, because the denial response has taken them to the point of no return."[10] It would seem that in one way or another, many congregations that have aligned themselves unthinkingly with the denomination's success or failure are in the same boat.

The nineties have been a time when we have found ourselves frightened by the earth tremors that have occurred as a result of the decay of received philosophical underpinnings and the lurching changes that are reshaping society as a whole. Consequently, instead of looking for creative and constructive ways forward, we have been hollering ever more frantically at one another from our little boats tossing around on a stormy sea. We have been engaged in a series of unwinnable political battles created, in part, by our determination to cling to opposite ends of yesterday's presuppositional spectrum.

I say unwinnable because not only are all the sides in the ecclesiastical power game squabbling to win outright control of a carcass left from the past, but when you play win-lose games in the church, ultimately everyone turns out to be the loser. One of my greatest fears is that we are going to start ripping our present structures apart in such a way that it turns into a bonanza for the legal eagles and a disaster for the Christian gospel. A fast growing conservative denomination, concerned for its own future, has been watching the Episcopal Church very carefully, not wishing to make some of the same mistakes. Their panel of experts has concluded that a wholesale breakup of the Episcopal Church would take fifty years to settle and would consume all of the church's assets in the payment of legal fees.

"See how these Christians love one another," the world will snigger, as expensive attorneys throw lawsuits at one another across crowded courtrooms.

The further erosion of Christian credibility will be enormous.

### Ecclesiastical War "Games"

In the early 1990s I made a firm prediction. I said that the final decade of the twentieth century would be one in which there would be "a lot of blood on the rug." I am sorry to say that my forecast has turned out to be even truer than I would ever have dreamed. As one who has studied with some care the religious conflicts (even wars) that resulted from the Reformation and who has then attempted to compare the past to the present, I find there are far too many parallels for comfort.

For example, many of the nastier items that have crossed my cyber-transom (from all sides of the interminable ecclesiastical debate) in the past few years have been strangely reminiscent of huge portions of the less edifying things that were said and written during the sixteenth and seventeenth centuries. The only thing we haven't yet taken to is burning one another at the stake!

Recall, for instance, some of the dreadful things that were being said in the lead-up to the English civil war, which began in 1642. At that time, the differences between Christian kings and nations resulted in protracted and bloody religious wars across the face of Europe. As controversy has swirled around the church today, particularly controversy focused on the topic of human sexuality, we have seen not only how the Internet can be used to advance causes, whether pro or con, but also the manner in which it has accelerated the metabolism of debate. Ideas that once took weeks to make it to each of the various players are now immediately in everyone's e-mail inbox.

Furthermore, because of its essentially strange mixture of the personal and the impersonal, the online process has intensified the polar-

ization that has been taking place. It is so much easier to slam someone
with whom you disagree when you are online because you don't have to
look them in the face and have them immediately respond. The bad
feeling engendered by such actions accumulates, poisoning the well of
good will until the final outcome is a total standoff, or a complete
turnoff.

One silver lining amidst all the clouds is that something appears to
be happening beneath the surface. This something suggests that while
seemingly intractable differences remain, a few, at least, are starting to
tire of the destructiveness and the mutual name-calling that has been
going on. Is this merely a lull in a battle that will keep erupting much as
the troubles in Ireland have over the last seven centuries? I do not know.

There are signs here and there that a few hardy souls are determined
to look for a more appropriate way out of the nastiness, but the jury is
out on whether they can succeed—or whether there is enough common ground to enable men and women of good will to find a way forward out of an apparently bitter stalemate. The question is whether we
will ever be able to treat our own pressing agenda items in such a way
that we seek the good of the whole rather than victory for our own particular cause.

### The Rise of Generation X

I sense that there could be a significant change of climate in the way we
handle controversy and divisiveness, as Generation X, those born approximately between JFK's assassination and Ronald Reagan's "morning in America," becomes a more important player on the American
church scene. This generation—many of whom are the pioneers of that
globally conscious age group about which we talked in the previous
chapter—is the first to have come to maturity within the postmodern
world, and given their experience, seem to have certain instincts that
could make them better able to handle the kind of tensions the with-
drawal of Modernity is leaving behind. This is not to say that Generation X, or any other generation for that matter, has all the answers, but
their attitudes could very well be a catalyst helping us to look at our circumstances from a different angle.

Generation Xers, rightly, "look upon themselves as pragmatic,
quick, sharp-eyed, able to step outside themselves to understand the
game of life as it really gets played."[11] As they see the polarization of the
churches, the Christians among them throw up their hands in horror

and lament the way the older generations are prepared to fight to the death over *their* issues.

A large portion of this generation of adults remember Mom and Dad, marriage in tatters, scrapping over who would get the house, who would pay the health insurance, and which one of them would get the custody of the children. A significant number of them are not happy to find the same dynamics at play in the life of the church. Perhaps they are going to be a kind of "clean-up" generation, able to hold the dangling threads of intense ambiguity together until these issues have worked themselves through. Some Generation X clergy, a small cadre in most of the mainline denominations, are talking about theirs as a generational "interim ministry."

However, in the old-line churches, of which the Episcopal Church is a prime example, where Generation X has been put firmly in its place and told until very recently that it is too young to worry its head about these things, we have literally robbed ourselves of the very people who might help us to manage our differences differently. Maybe our unwillingness until the last year or two to take seriously the call to leadership of those born after the mid-sixties reflects an organism in denial, and therefore in acute crisis. The result of our shortsightedness is that we are now woefully lacking the critical mass of younger priests and layleaders needed if we are to have anything approaching a healthy future.

Based on the current situation, research suggests that in the Episcopal Church alone we need to be training in one way or another, 5,000 to 7,500 new members of the clergy in the next twelve to fifteen years. Most of them will need to be younger rather than older, and a significant proportion will require the sort of entrepreneurial skills that will enable them to revive flagging congregations, plant new parishes, and develop new ministries. While dioceses are, here and there, starting to pick up on this, I fear that seminaries are, for the most part, not only trapped by yesterday's way of perceiving belief, but are also still over-enamored by the sixties way of being the church. Much of the present configuration of our seminaries is no longer appropriate for training people for ordained and lay leadership.

### Too Irrelevant?

But there is another pressing reality: Denominations as presently configured have become less and less relevant. A few remaining leaders from the World War II generation and a whole bevy of "Silents" (that is, those born between the mid-1920s and mid-1940s) maintain their control of mainline denominational structures, preserving the hierarchical, centralized structures they received from the past—regardless of their relevance to today's world. Leonard Sweet puts it more colorfully, "Part of the church's deficiency is bad plumbing. In the modern world, denominational pipes channeled in the living water to the thirsty."[12] But the delivery system created by denominational machines is coming undone. Not only are structures showing considerable wear and tear, they are unlikely to last very long in their present format once Boomers become the controlling majority. Boomers are likely to begin the process of networking the churches that Generation X will take the next step.

In 1997, a Boomer friend and I sat in on a hearing at the Episcopal Church's General Convention in Philadelphia that dealt with the issue of apportionment of funding from dioceses to the National Church. We listened with increasing despondency as a group of people predominantly in their late fifties to early seventies coolly trotted out the old saw that giving up the line to the central structures was a test of loyalty, thus every diocese should cough up 21 percent for the national budget. My friend, a respected priest and thoughtful church leader, turned to me and we both said to each other at the same time, "What planet do these people live on?"

The plan they had hatched was subsequently endorsed by a gray-haired convention, but it has been treated in a somewhat cavalier manner by a good number of Boomer-controlled diocesan conventions. It illustrated a total misunderstanding of what drives and shapes the thinking of those under fifty. For Boomers and Generation Xers, issues of loyalty to a tottering denominational structure are peripheral to much more significant issues of accountability. These generations have limited patience with hierarchies of any kind and are much more at home with decentralized networks, informal linkages, and flatter organizational styles. Within the next few years it is these folks who will predominate in most ecclesial structures, and then we are likely to see them placing their own imprint on the way the church does business.

While it is hard to know what this might look like, we can be certain that it will be very different from what we have in place now. Effective denominational structures in the future will be those that function more as supportive networks for those at the front line—the congregations—than hierarchies of control. Visionary denominational entities will be those that develop and provide to their parishes the finest resources available for congregational growth and mission. It will require the cultivation of significant knowledge bases, as well as the nurture of the right kind of personnel. This will require careful planning and the commitment of significant dollars to the task, but the fruits could be considerable.

### Back to Tradition

Meanwhile, paradoxically, even as the formal structures are showing signs of being worn out and of limited value, we are seeing a rapidly emerging predisposition among younger Christians to treasure the richness that has been contained in the dilapidated old wineskins in which various Christian traditions have been stored. The young, who have been brought up in a world that has been unreflectively disposing of most of the fortunes of past rootedness, are now out there picking over this so-called "rubbish" from the past, initially out of curiosity. To their surprise, they are discovering treasures about which they are becoming very enthusiastic.

While they are unlikely to restore the organizational patterns of the mid-twentieth century, it is highly likely that as they forage through the basements and attics of the church, deep but forgotten spiritual riches from the diversity of classic Christian traditions will pour back into the church's life. Could it be that we will see testings of the waters and the experimental mingling of old and new that will eventually lead us out of our present "captivity" into a series of different kinds of ecclesiastical affiliations, each of which is deeply rooted in one or another aspect of Christian tradition?

Robert E. Webber, an Episcopal layperson and professor of theology, recently wrote,

> The kind of Christianity that attracts the new generation of Christians and will speak effectively to a Postmodern world is one that emphasizes primary truths and authentic embodiment. The new generation is more interested in broad strokes than detail, more attracted to an inclusive view of the faith than an exclusive view, more concerned with unity than diversity, more open to a dynamic, growing faith than a static fixed system, and more visual than verbal with a high level of tolerance and ambiguity. It is at these points that the link between the ancient tradition and the new generation can be made. The early tradition of the faith dealt with basic issues, and was concerned with unity, open and dynamic, mystical, relational, visual, and tangible.[13]

In light of the roiling brew that the churches have become in the last fifteen years, the first half of the twenty-first century could well be an era in which perhaps six or seven different families of Christian traditions, configured entirely differently from what we have now, will emerge. These are likely to be built around differing sets of commonality than what has prevailed in our recent past, and the linkages between Christians might be novel and somewhat different from what we have seen before. It is entirely likely that they will be focused more upon our ability to undertake Christian mission with integrity, and in cooperation with one another, than those ideas, doctrines, ethnicities, and issues that previously separated us.

These configurations are likely to be much more horizontally rather than hierarchically ordered. Following the advice of elder statesmen like Lyle E. Schaller, and bearing in mind that people today are more likely to organize by affinity, they could be less geographically bounded in the traditional sense, require less formal infrastructure, and be judicatories and dioceses affiliating with one another on entirely different grounds than just locality.[14]

During the 1990s we saw a bewildering array of congregations switching horses midstream, so that independent charismatic fellowships are becoming Orthodox parishes, and even in these difficult times, there are congregations as a whole interested in joining the Episcopal Church. All these twists and turns may, for the denomination, develop into the kinds of Christian connection that will provide the environment and structure for the re-evangelization of the West.

Let me end this chapter with some words of Will Willimon, Chaplain of Duke University. Willimon, speaking from the perspective of the risen Christ addressing the old-line, mainline denominations:

> Your marginalization may be providential. I promise you renewal, not restoration. Many will be grateful for your mainline open-handedness, the way you manage to make room for such a wide range of faithfulness within your congregations, your confidence that the church is more than an isolated congregation, that I ought to have a Body, and that the witness of the Saints is worth celebrating today.
>
> Personally, I think you tend to be open-minded to a fault. Latitudinarianism is you all over. I wish you would hire some theologians with some guts for a change. Can't you find something more fun to do than General Assemblies, General Conferences, and Diocesan Conventions? Some of your good ideas

from the last century may need a decent burial if I can work birth in you in the next.

One more thing. Please get out of the middle of the road! That's where all the accidents happen, theologically speaking. Remember, I wasn't crucified for my moderation.[15]

✦ ✦ ✦

### To Think and Talk Over

1. Reread and ponder the quote from Dr. Loren Mead that is to be found at the beginning of this chapter.
2. What ecumenical initiatives have you found encouraging, and which have you found discouraging in recent years?
3. Is there too much poison and vitriol in church systems for there to be reconciliation? Are we more likely to splinter than to stay to-gether—and why?
4. As you look at your parish, diocese, or judicatory how much are their actions shaped by a call to mission and how much are they shaped by a denial of realities?
5. Is it possible to train 5,000 to 7,500 new leaders in the next fifteen years in a church like the Episcopal Church?
6. Study Jesus' teaching about unity in St. John's Gospel, chapter 17.

### Suggestions for Further Reading

Campolo, Tony. *Can Mainline Denominations Make a Comeback?* (Valley Forge, PA: Judson Press, 1995).

Hutcheson, Richard G., Jr., and Shriver, Peggy. *The Divided Church: Moving Liberals and Conservatives from Diatribe to Dialogue* (Downers Grove, IL: InterVarsity Press, 1999).

Humphery, Nathan (ed.). *Gathering the Next Generation* (Harrisburg, PA: Morehouse Publishing, 2000).

Keck, Leander. *The Church Confident* (Nashville, TN: Abingdon Press, 1993).

Kew, Richard, and White, Roger J. *Toward 2015—A Church Odyssey* (Boston: Cowley Publications, 1997).

Mead, Loren B. *The Once and Future Church* (Washington, D.C.: The Alban Institute, 1991).

Schaller, Lyle E. *Tattered Trust* (Nashville, TN: Abingdon Press, 1997).

Shenk, Wilbert R. *Write the Vision* (Valley Forge, PA: Trinity Press International, 1995).

Sine, Tom. *Cease Fire—Searching for Sanity in America's Culture Wars* (Grand Rapids, MI: Wm. B. Eerdmans Publishing Co., 1995).

Snyder, Howard A. *EarthCurrents: The Struggle for the World's Soul* (Nashville, TN: Abingdon Press, 1995).

Sweet, Leonard. *SoulTsunami* (Grand Rapids, MI: Zondervan. 1998).

Sweet, Leonard. *AquaChurch* (Loveland, Co: Group Publishing, 1999).

### Web Sites

- Leonard Sweet is a one-man Christian futures industry. Of his various ventures, his sites www.leonardsweet.com and www.soultsumani.com are worth a visit. They are full of resources and ideas for groups seeking to understand how the church is being reworked.
- The Leadership Network's Web site is a goldmine of resources to help you understand what has been happening. It can be reached at www.leadnet.org.
- A helpful Web site for understanding the differences in the generations is the *Reaching the Generations for Jesus* site that can be found at http://home.pix.za/gc/gc12.
- While you are there, go on and look at the Young Leaders' Network, which links to the Leadership Network at www.youngleader.org.

# TREND THREE
# The Future Lies with Mission-Driven Units

*The Christian churches cannot rely on a legacy of cultural religiosity to ensure their continued presence in the world. They must proclaim the profound attractiveness of faith to the world, in the full and confident expectation that the gospel is inherently attractive and relevant.*[1]
Alister McGrath, theologian, writer, and seminary dean

### Back to the Fifties

During the last quarter century, innumerable words have been written about the church needing to shed some of yesterday's restraints and become mission-driven, rather than continuing to plod unimaginatively on in the maintenance mindset. Despite all that has been said, and despite all the changes within our culture, most congregations continue to function as if this were the middle of the twentieth century, rather than the beginning of the twenty-first.

Since old habits die hard, we find it difficult to let go of our pastorally obsessed ways of being church, which we inherited from a fast-departing Christendom. No matter how well we comprehend this, the vast majority of congregations of just about every denomination seem virtually incapable of breaking the old mold. Episcopal intransigence on the matter sounds much like that of Southern Baptists, Methodists, or just about any other tradition. We are all in the same boat together.

The idyllic model for which we nostalgically yearn in the Anglican tradition, of which I am part, is the village church of the days of yore, with the priest as jolly "parson. There are far too many of these jovial "parsons" avuncularly ministering to dwindling and aging flocks, while making little or no impact for the gospel within their communities. Some priests seem to deliberately cultivate or even accentuate this somewhat eccentric side of their personalities. As picturesque as this might seem, quaint clergy are not the tradition, but one of the barnacles the tradition has gathered. These barnacles are not just slowing the ship. Unless we can modify our approach to ministry, they are likely to take the ship down with them—crew and all.

### A Whisper of Evangelism

However, there are some encouraging signs. When Roger White and I wrote about the future of the Episcopal Church in *New Millennium, New Church* a decade ago, we described evangelism as the "dreaded *e* word in the Episcopal Church." To say the word *evangelism* in Episcopal settings was like shouting "Fire!" in a theater. It was wise not to be too close to the door, because you could have been trampled underfoot by the crowd as it fought to get out! Evangelism is now far less of an embarrassment these days among North American Anglicans, with even some of the least likely bishops calling for significant advancement and church growth.

This may be the eleventh hour in the old mainline churches, but even the eleventh hour is not necessarily too late. It is exciting that we are beginning to take church planting seriously, and also that tools like Alpha and Emmaus have made a considerable difference in people's sensibilities.[2] For whatever reason, judicatories that have had little involvement in the arena of evangelism are now talking seriously about mission, evangelism, and church growth. The cynic would suggest that this is because numbers are shrinking and the bills need to be paid, but perhaps another reason is that God's Spirit is at work!

Yet what is most puzzling is that such a large number of the old-line seminaries are lagging far behind local congregations. Few of them have started taking mission and evangelism with the seriousness necessary for the church to survive—let alone thrive—in the future. This failure is due in part to the academic captivity of theological education where those who train tomorrow's leaders are increasingly removed from the general ebb-and-flow of parish life and are following an entirely different agenda. It also illustrates how far we still have to go—just talking about mission and evangelism is not enough.

Given that seminary culture is almost hermetically sealed off from the parochial grass roots it is no wonder that we are so overwhelmed by a multitude of backward-looking "parsons," because the culture of so many of the seminaries is designed to form people as such. The "parson" model has been modernized and intensified by what one friend of mine calls the seminaries' "obsession with therapeutic models of ministry." Add to this the fact much education for Christian leadership is driven by an anemic and outmoded latitudinarian theology, and it is possible to see some of the causes of this pickle.

A few forward-looking leaders are encouraging the church to rethink the way it functions in this fast-emerging secular-pagan world of the twenty-first century. However, we are only at the front end of a long and demanding re-engineering process, and many more will have to get on board for there to be real momentum in this direction. We have to be prepared to take the risks and be willing to make the kinds of mistakes that go with launching out in faith in a visionary manner. All but a relative handful have hunkered down and are functioning in a survivalist mode.

Those engaged in aggressively transforming the church through evangelism would be quick to say that the line on the graph is not going to rise rapidly, and that even they have a long way to go. Judicatories going in this direction have been spending the last few years just clearing the ground and planting the seeds for the future; it will be a generation down the road before we will begin to see whether their efforts are bearing long-term fruit. It takes time and effort to turn a vessel around, especially if it is plying its way through choppy seas.

One of the priorities right now is merely to reverse the spirit of inertia and timidity that prevails almost everywhere. For example, Bishop Claude Payne of the Episcopal Diocese of Texas began his episcopate by audaciously challenging his sizable diocese to double during the coming ten years. To focus in the right direction has taken considerable effort and strong leadership from the bishop and his staff. Others concerned for the future of the old-line churches are beginning to recognize that leadership involves not just issuing the challenge, but providing the resources for congregations and judicatories to change direction and move forward.

One Episcopal bishop, Dan Herzog of Albany, New York, when addressing his first diocesan convention as the bishop, told the shocked gathering that the hour is late and the situation dire. After having pointed out that between 1983–98, the diocese had lost 14,000 people, or 38 percent of its membership, and then having followed this through with an equally depressing list of other statistics told his listeners, "It is my considered judgment that as a diocese we have about four years to reverse our decline or we will face catastrophic results. Already I visit parishes where the youngest person is sixty and a decade of funerals will wipe it out. If these parishes die, we aren't able to do CPR on a corpse. We need to do it now—to restore them to life."[3]

These were strong words. But the bishop did not just issue them as a scolding condemnation; he has backed them up with the kind of visionary leadership that is needed to radically alter course. Bishop Herzog, for example, has been enthusiastically and actively involved in the introduction and development of the internationally renowned Alpha course as a primary tool for congregational renewal in his diocese, which stretches along the eastern flank of New York state. Since talking in these terms, the Diocese of Albany has begun to turn around.

### Breaking the Christendom Habit

Breaking deeply ingrained, 1,500-year-old Christendom habits requires extraordinary re-education and enormous effort. Bishop Herzog, for example, is in the process of establishing the mindset in the Episcopal Diocese of Albany that they are first and foremost a missionary entity and can no longer afford to be cute little Episcopal chaplaincies. Much of the church is, as yet, unprepared to even consider, let alone begin making the effort necessary to re-create the church so that while remaining rooted and grounded in the richness of its past, it will be oriented to be missionary into its future.

There has been an enormous amount of talk about and experience of spiritual renewal in the last thirty years, but often that renewal has meant little more than brightening up worship, swapping sentimental Victorian music for sappy twentieth-century tunes and lyrics, and listening to preachers who might be a little more in touch with the central and substantial truths of the gospel but do not know how to present the Word of God in an edifying manner so that it might nourish their hungry congregations. But renewal has another side. "Renewal," writes Alister McGrath, Principal of Wycliffe College, Oxford, "may well mean a painful process of self-examination, in which many cherished ideas and approaches of the past are set on one side as redundant and unhelpful."[4]

If the twenty-first-century church is to have an effective future, it has to realize that it is being called to make radical and fundamental changes—what will amount to a profound and deep paradigm shift. In the last couple of years, Kevin Martin, Canon for Congregational Development in the Diocese of Texas, and I conceived a plan that might help us do this. We decided to develop a growing team of change agents. The task of these agents is to be successfully able to lead their own parishes as they attempt to make the leap from a tired Christendom to a dynamic missionary model of being church—and then to coach and encourage others as they make the same moves. Although this project is still very much at the experimental stage, we think we are beginning to discover how to develop the kinds of tools that will help us as we adapt to a very different kind of world.[5]

Despite these forays in the right direction, I fear that the real drive to rethink seriously what it means to be a missionary church will only come in North America in response to some kind of major crisis. Just about the only crisis that catches the attention of parishes and dioceses is a steep decline in church attendance (and resulting revenues), which then threatens the church's actual survival. While this may not be the most worthy of motives, if it serves as an effective wake-up call, let the numbers hit us like a two-by-four to get our attention.

During the last few years, I have seen the beginnings of a willingness to "think outside the box" when membership and revenue numbers spiral downward. This has been especially the case in parts of the Northeast, West, and many regions in Canada. While I applaud those who have seen the writing on the wall, it is still possible that the remedy might have come too late for many congregations, and even entire judicatories. It is entirely conceivable that the first half of this century will see at least 60 percent of all congregations now in existence in North America close their doors forever.

### No Longer Such a Churchgoing Nation

On the basis of polling data from both the Gallup and the Barna organizations, it has been generally believed for many years that 35–40 percent of Americans are on any one Sunday involved in church life. More recent and more focused research is beginning to suggest that church attendance may not be this high. It would appear that the size of the sample along with the nature and depth of past polling has not been adequate, and this has over inflated the resulting attendance figures. One theory posited for this is that people have a tendency to tell pollsters what they think the questioner wants to hear rather than giving correct details of what is being investigated.

I live in a part of the U.S.A. that is supposed to have significantly higher than average church attendance each Sunday—in the region of 60–70 percent. While it is true that membership rolls in the South are huge, and that attendance is higher than elsewhere, just looking at church attendance patterns in the neighborhood in which I live sug-

gests that these figures are grossly inflated. While I know that it is un-
wise to argue from the particular to the general, all I need to do is look
at my own street in the vicinity of a state university as a sample. I would
be very surprised if the number of residents who regularly turn out to
church each Sunday reached the 25 percent level.[6]

If we accept the traditional figures, then "each month," according to
George Barna, "Christian churches come into contact with 100 million
adults and more than thirty million children." If the numbers are exaggerated, then the real count is likely to be proportionately lower—but
still far larger than most other developed nations. Unfortunately, however many churches there are, "most of them are involved in a religious
ritual," Barna observes, "and have little connection with Christ."

If by "Christian" one means that someone has a life-transforming
encounter with the gospel that has eternal consequences for both this
life and the life to come, then Barna's studies reveal that one-half of
those in contact with the church lack the substance of Christian convictions. Many are essentially little more than secular beings who attend
religious services either out of habit or for a variety of reasons that may
be unclear even to them. The Barna research reckons that only 10–15
percent of the nation's 320,000 churches can be rated "highly effective"
in the way they form their membership in Christ. Postmodern Christianity is chock-full of "religious" men and women with little faith in
Christ—"'Christian agnostics,' if you will."[7] This information should be
giving us pause for thought.

While there are regions in which churchgoing has declined consid-
erably, many parts of the U.S.A. are still able to cultivate a strong
churchgoing tradition. The Old South, for example, probably has the
highest levels of church attendance and other religious observance of
anywhere in the Western world. Yet if the radical spiritual diversification of the culture is anything to go by, this is changing. Nevertheless,
while the pews are still being warmed, it means that many will be quite
content to rest on their laurels for some considerable time to come.

What is encouraging is to see the way the church in other parts of
the Western world, where slippage of attendance has been precipi-
tous, is waking up to the circumstances in which it finds itself. Despite
sometimes pitiful numbers, there is a fascinating degree of both en-
thusiasm and creativity in countries like Britain and New Zealand;
each of these lands is far further down the secular-pagan road than
the U.S.A.

At a recent interdenominational gathering of young church leaders
I attended, all in their twenties and early thirties, the internationals

from other parts of the Western world were much more creative and exciting than the majority of the home-grown Generation Xers. Interestingly, while these internationals were the most creative, they were also the ones most likely to be rooted in the traditions of the classic Christianity that developed during the first five centuries of the Christian faith.

### Talking Evangelism More Than Doing Evangelism and Mission

Another disheartening element is our unwillingness to be proactive in mission and evangelism. Thankfully we are starting to get over our fear of talking about evangelism and the mission of the church, but now we have to take the next step toward active strategizing and creative implementation. This means changing the way in which both parishes and dioceses order their priorities.

North American Anglicanism, like all the other mainline traditions, has customarily been much more enthusiastic about social causes and the great systemic issues of the day. In addition, we have tended to work with the unspoken assumption that our society still operates as part of Christendom, and that the movers and shakers are bound to listen attentively to what we have to say. This is no longer the case, and while it is important that the churches play a role in pricking the nation's conscience, let us not pretend that those who shape national or the local community's life are necessarily going to give serious consideration to our concerns and causes.

Quite honestly, for several generations now our eyes have been focused more on "the issues" than on Jesus. This has meant that mainline Christians have tended to become numb to the prodding to strategize, pray, give, go out, and act selflessly in the work of evangelism and mission. If we are to thrive in the coming millennium the church needs to create the ecclesiastical equivalent of a "war economy," with the mission of the church focused around the business of proclaiming the saving grace that is ours in Jesus Christ—rather than these other important, but peripheral activities.

This is not to say that social transformation is unimportant. Rather, social transformation is not going to happen unless hearts and minds are transformed by the indwelling power of God through the living Spirit. The starting point for Christian witness and action is the covenant relationship that God makes with the people God has chosen. Their desire to reach out to meet the needs of society will inevitably flow from this personal relationship with the Holy One.

Wilbert R. Shenk, a Mennonite scholar and missiologist who teaches at Fuller Theological Seminary, offers the following challenge to churches like our own:

> The church's understanding of itself, the gospel, and the world is always reflected in the content and manner of its evangelization. At no other point does the church place itself so openly at cross-purposes with the world than when it announces that this present order has no efficacious answer to human destiny. If the church, under the inspiration of its head, Jesus Christ, lives by the conviction that the world is on a course that leads to death, it has no other choice than to invite men and women to become part of God's new order, the kingdom of life. The church that is not evangelizing is a church that does not truly believe the gospel. It is a faithless church.[8]

Right now, substantial elements of the North American churches need to be asking themselves whether they truly believe the gospel. We have significant resources, more than most churches in the world, but so often we are taking them and pouring them into areas of work that are tangential to the primary missionary task. Instead, we need to be focusing time, treasure, and talent in large quantities upon the business of proclaiming Christ and forming new believers in him.

I grew up in Britain, a country that had spent the seven years immediately prior to my birth fighting for its life. The "war economy" that had been in force meant that every conceivable asset the nation and its people possessed was focused on winning the war. My homeland had literally drained its coffers and borrowed heavily in order to defeat Adolf Hitler and the Nazi menace. While my early years were not *that* uncomfortable, we did not have many luxuries because the country now had to rebuild after channeling everything into that effort. It was to take about a decade and a half to dismantle this way of using resources. The time has come for us carefully to examine all that we do as parishes, dioceses, and as a national church, abandoning those activities and diversions that lead us away from our primary task.

The Episcopal Church, for example, at its General Convention held in Denver in July 2000, committed to doubling its numbers by 2020.[9] Other denominations have entered the new millennium with similar far-reaching and admirable dreams. However, such goals will not be reached without a fundamental and radical reorientation of priorities—and considerable sacrifice. We need to ask whether we are willing to work not only to reach out to those beyond the Kingdom, that they may become part of our Christian communities, but also whether we are prepared to help them form themselves in Jesus Christ so that they become real disciples. This will require time, much talent, and a lot of resources—both financial and otherwise. Traditionally, mainline churches have expected low levels of commitment from their members, but now we must reverse this approach and develop the highest expectations of converts to Jesus Christ as they are enfolded in our congregations.

Another component of reaching this goal must be the planting of new churches. Again, until the last few years the older denominations have lagged far behind newer and more conservative churches in this. During the last quarter of the twentieth century, the Episcopal Church planted a mere 300–400 new congregations. All the mainline churches have statistics that show new congregations were enthusiastically planted in the burgeoning suburbs in the twenty years following World War II, but this then slowed to a mere trickle between the mid-sixties and the mid-nineties.

Yet the fact is that the unchurched are reached not so much through existing parishes, but through new ones that have the capacity to take the good news of Jesus Christ into different social and relational networks. Those of us who are Anglicans need to set ourselves to establish *at least* 2,500–3,000 new congregations during the first two decades of the new millennium if we are to stay where we are to maintain our numbers, let alone grow. What is true for our tradition is equally true for those in the other churches.

It is important that our existing congregations learn how to welcome people into their fellowship and that they discover how to provide these outsiders with opportunities both to know Christ personally and to grow in their Christian faith. This will mean rethinking the way we approach new member incorporation, confirmation, baptism preparation, and all those other various rites of passage that cluster around the life of a parish.

Henri Nouwen hit the nail on the head when he said, "If there is any concept worth restoring to its original depth and evocative potential, it is the concept of hospitality,"[10] and it is this mindset that needs to undergird our approach to mission and evangelism—we are to live with our arms wide open, welcoming people in. "Hospitality is the lens through which we can read and understand much of the gospel, and a practice by which we can welcome Jesus himself," comments Christine Pohl, Professor of Social Ethics at Asbury Theological Seminary,

Wilmore, Kentucky. "Recovering hospitality as a vital aspect of Christian life will be more complex than simply resurrecting an old-fashioned practice . . . The contemporary church hungers for models of a more authentic Christian life in which glimpses of the Kingdom can be seen and the promise of the Kingdom can be embodied."[11]

A church's capacity to welcome people is an important gauge of its potential to grow both in grace and numbers. In addition, it means that leaders should know not only how to share their faith meaningfully, but how to communicate the capacity and excitement of this to others. Given our current state of affairs, we have a lot of work ahead of us, if we intend to recover and excel in the exercise of the Christian virtue of hospitality.

### Christians and the Culture

Furthermore, when we look around the churches, it seems that most eyes are blind to the changing realities within the wider culture. Not everyone shares the conviction that we are moving into a post-Christian world. One prominent Episcopal leader recently scolded me for supposing that as Postmodernity advances, society is becoming ever more secular and pagan—and, as a result, at odds with Christianity. However, I have been monitoring an array of cultural indicators for a long time, and the present trend toward secularism intermingled with a distinctly non-Christian approach to spirituality looks set to prevail.

As I have gone over these indicators again and again, they all suggested that pluralism and immense religious diversity are advancing at an incredible rate. Pluralism in its very essence is a comprehensive reworking of the Christian roots of our Western past. If we refuse to accept this emerging reality, and do not distinctly begin relating to this changing world cross-culturally and as missionaries, then it is only a matter of time before we have completely removed ourselves from the conversation, in effect rendering ourselves utterly irrelevant. During the next ten years we will increasingly see the winnowing effects of this changing climate.

Even if the church does not divide and reconfigure itself thorough schism and recoalescing along different theological and organizational lines, we are bound to see marginal dioceses and judicatories ceasing to be viable—some are already perilously close to the edge and others are bound to follow, despite their assets and endowments. Furthermore, it can be expected that increasing numbers of congregations will be forced to downsize (whether that be in terms of physical plant or personnel), due to what comes with an aging population: fewer parishioners and less money upon which to survive.

In some places these pressures are already upon the churches, especially rural areas in the prairie states. The situation has become so critical in certain places where there is massive population decline that even *The New York Times* published a major article dealing with the issue, focusing on North Dakota. Given the importance of churches as centers for community life in sparsely populated areas, this piece was deeply concerned about the effect of declining numbers and dollars upon the viability of churches in such areas.[12]

It is sad to see a store post "going out of business" sale notices. When huge chain stores like Wal-Mart and Books-A-Million set up shop in Murfreesboro, Tennessee, where I live, there was a rash of such closings as smaller competitors gave up the struggle and chose liquidation over bankruptcy. When a church goes through the process of going out of business, sadness is magnified. It is as hard to hear as it is to say it, but the signs indicate that there will be an increase in the number of parishes going out of business during the coming decade, from a few isolated cases to churches being closed in large multiples—much as the Roman Catholics have had to do in major industrial cities like Detroit in recent years.

Peter Wagner, who has studied and taught church growth at Fuller Theological Seminary, Pasadena, California, for many years, recently estimated that right now approximately 18,000 of the 300,000 Protestant churches in the U.S.A. are probably "terminally ill." While some might possibly be treated and cured, the majority are likely to go out of existence. "Churches die hard," Professor Wagner writes. "Many of them go out kicking and screaming, so to speak, and bring little blessing to the kingdom of God in the process."[13]

If this seems depressing, the future is bright for those congregations that are willing to grapple with the changing environment and are prepared to reorient themselves so that they are Christ-centered and mission-driven. Those congregations and judicatories that are committed to proclamation at worst will survive, and at best will prosper. The same is true for those seminaries (and other approaches to theological education) that train men and women for leadership in these altered circumstances, reconfiguring themselves in the process. The question that many of our seminaries need to be asking themselves is whether they are going to use their often-considerable endowments just to stay in business, or whether they are going to retool themselves to be centers from which the whole people of God can be equipped to do the whole ministry of God.

Perhaps a model that mainline seminaries should consider is Northern Baptist Theological Seminary in Lombard, Illinois. While remaining part of the American Baptist denomination, it has over the years gathered a faculty from across the ecclesial spectrum, and it seeks to serve the spread of the Gospel way beyond its own church environs. In the last few years they have developed a strong relationship with the Willow Creek Association of churches, built around the "seeker-sensitive" approach to ministry pioneered by Willow Creek Church in South Barrington, Illinois. Meanwhile, they have added Robert E. Webber, an Episcopal academic, to their faculty. Webber was attracted to the school because "Northern's commitment to develop a new kind of seminary education to prepare men and women for ministry in a postmodern world is visionary and compelling."

I have been ordained more than thirty years, have visited for ministry most of the dioceses of the Episcopal Church and a number other Anglican provinces. I have gone to well over 750 Episcopal churches in one capacity or another in Canada and abroad, and have in differing ways served in six congregations on two continents. These congregations have covered the waterfront, from wealthy suburban provinces to a rural mission in Appalachia. While all those churches have had their struggles and challenges, I can honestly say that I have *never* been part of a congregation that has shrunk. Hopefully, the primary reason for this is that Jesus is being lifted up in a meaningful way.

As I hear from my contemporaries from seminary—most of us nearer the end than the beginning of our ministries and sharing the same mission-oriented mindset as myself—few are depressed and many are seeing considerable growth and blessing in parishes, even those working in the hardest parts of Britain's decaying industrial cities. These are not individuals who are burned out and are counting off the days to their first pension check, but folks who are genuinely excited by the Gospel, and the way it transforms lives and the world. The Good News has not lost its power in their lives, nor its magnetic appeal to those who were once beyond the reach of the church, but are now committed believers in their congregations. It is as we recover our excitement with the message and respond appropriately and creatively that we will see God doing extraordinary things.

While I am certain that the twenty-first century will hardly be all smooth sailing, if the church is to survive and thrive its primary task must be the Great Commission. Churches with that emphasis will be blessed both numerically and in other ways.

+ + +

### To Think and Talk Over

1. Does your parish have a mission and evangelism strategy?
2. What do you look for most in a candidate to be rector/vicar/pastor of the parish—a good pastoral manner, or the gifts that can help the congregation grow the church?
3. How would you begin developing an evangelistic strategy for your parish? How do you think this would be accepted by the various groups within the congregation?
4. Would you say that your congregation is made up more of mere attendees than genuine disciples? If the answer is yes, then what sort of moves need to be made to rectify the situation?
5. Consider the unchurched in your area. Think about what it would be like if your parish were to plant a new congregation. How would you go about it, and what impact do you think it would have on both the existing congregation and the neighborhood?
6. For a pastor to be equipped for ministry in the twenty-first century, what skills and topics ought to be taught at seminary?

### Suggestions for Further Reading

Allen, Roland. *Missionary Methods: St. Paul's or Ours?* (Grand Rapids, MI: Wm. B. Eerdman Publishing Co., 1962).

Allen, Roland. *The Spontaneous Expansion of the Church* (Grand Rapids, MI: Wm. B. Eerdman Publishing Co., 1962).

Green, Michael. *Evangelism in the Early Church* (London: Hodder and Stoughton, 1968).

Hunter, George G., III. *How to Reach Secular People* (Nashville, TN: Abingdon Press, 1993).

Hunter, George G., III. *The Celtic Way of Evangelism* (Nashville, TN: Abingdon Press, 2000).

Payne, Claude E. *Reclaiming the Great Commission: A Practical Model for Transforming Denominations and Congregations* (San Francisco: Jossey-Bass, 2000).

Sweet, Leonard. *FaithQuakes* (Nashville, TN: Abingdon Press, 1994).

Shenk, Wilbert R. *Write the Vision—The Church Renewed* (Valley Forge, PA: Trinity Press International, 1995).

Wagner, C. Peter. *The Healthy Church* (Ventura, CA: Regal Books, 1996).

Warren, Rick. *The Purpose-Driven Church* (Grand Rapids, MI: Zondervan, 1995).

### Web Sites

- The Web Site of the Episcopal Network for Evangelism has some good ideas and excellent links. It can be found at http://members.aol.com/ENE2020/.
- *American Demographics* is a publication that says a lot about the culture in which we are ministering. Their Web Site is http://www.demographics.com/.
- There are all sorts of Episcopal and Anglican related mission and evangelism choices at the www.episcopalian.org Web site.
- The Reverend Beth Maynard talks a lot about communicating with post-Boomer Generations on her Web site that can be reached at http://get.to/pomo. She also does some careful describing of the characteristics of the various generations.
- Rick Warren of Saddleback Church in California has put together a Web site entitled www.pastors.com, which could be extremely helpful to many of our congregations as they seek new ways forward.
- A number of Anglicans have been greatly helped by the wider church planting movement. The site of the Church Multiplication Training Center has much to offer. It can be found at www.cmtcmultiply.org/team.htm.
- If you want to find out more about Northern Baptist Theological Seminary, then you will find them at www.seminary.edu. As a friend of mine has pointed out, just the name of their Web site suggests that these folk saw the way the world was going and got in there first!

# TREND FOUR
# A Growing Mound of Major Fiscal Challenges

*Any "Christian" who takes for himself anything more than the "plain necessaries of life," (John) Wesley insisted, "lives in an open, habitual denial of the Lord." He has "gained riches and hell-fire!" Wesley lived what he preached. Sales of his books often earned him 1,400 pounds annually, but he spent only thirty pounds on himself. The rest he gave away. He always wore inexpensive clothes and dined on simple food. "If I leave behind me ten pounds," he once wrote, "you and all mankind bear witness against me that I lived and died a thief and a robber!"*[1]

Ronald J. Sider, professor, writer, and Christian activist

### Benefits of the Boom

If the nineties had not produced such a booming economy in the U.S.A., without doubt the nation's longest sustained period of economic growth and prosperity in its history, it is highly likely that some really nasty fiscal problems would already be roiling the waters for the churches. In Canada, where the economy has not been so resurgent, where the value of the currency has been depressed, where bitter lawsuits have dogged the churches, and where the bite of secularism and neopaganism has been deep, this is already happening.[2]

At a time when there is so much money sloshing around in the American system, even the most unhealthy Christian units, whether judicatories or congregations, can be made to look fitter than they really are—for a while. And, of course, it helps if you have endow-

ments that have done very well in the great bull market of the last
decade of the last century, as have many of the institutions of the
older denominations.

One of the greatest Wall Street investors of the twentieth century is
Sir John Templeton. Now an old man with a rich legacy, his life can be
a parable for us. Born into a relatively modest but devout Presbyterian
home in Winchester, Tennessee, he has for many years been both a res-
ident and a citizen of the Bahamas—thus his knighthood. He prides
himself that he borrowed money only once in his life, having worked
his way through Harvard on a shoestring budget during the dark years
of the thirties, and then winning a Rhodes scholarship to Oxford. As
the clouds of war began to threaten in 1939, by now an impecunious
Wall Streeter, he managed to persuade one of his relatively well-to-do
uncles to lend him $10,000. This he invested in penny stocks—of which
there were scads during that Depression-colored era.

It was his thesis that America would inevitably become the engine
of the West's battle against Hitler, whether the U.S.A. joined the war or
not, and that even the most incompetent of companies would thrive in
such an environment. He was right—only two of the several hundred
corporations that he bet upon failed to stay afloat. Templeton made a
bumper profit on the others—and a great investing "empire" was born
that would play a significant role in funding and shaping the post-war
world.[3] Sir John's uncle got his money back posthaste, and Templeton
went on to become one of the richest (and most generous) Christian
men in the world.

I tell this story because the comfortable financial environment of
the last few years has, like the prospects of war in Europe for Templeton, made it easier for significant numbers of marginal parishes to find
the dollars to keep the roof on, the doors open, and the pastor paid.
When people are feeling fat and prosperous, churches, which have
during the Christendom era traditionally been the recipients of at least
a portion of even their most fringe members' discretionary giving, are
going to share the fruits. However, when the downturn comes, even if
giving to religious causes stays relatively buoyant compared to certain
other charitable causes, churches are often among the first to feel a
chill breeze.

Many believe that it will be a long time before such a wind starts to
blow. Peter Schwartz, one of the most thoughtful commercial futurists,
one of the few who foresaw the great oil crisis of the early seventies, has
long been optimistic and bullish about the world's economic future. In
1998 he wrote, "We are watching the beginnings of a global economic

boom on a scale never experienced before. We have entered a period of sustained growth that could eventually double the world's economy every dozen years and bring prosperity for—quite literally—billions of people on the planet. We are riding the early waves of a twenty-five-year run of a greatly expanding economy that will do much to solve seemingly intractable problems like poverty and to ease tensions throughout the world."[4]

Yet not everyone shares Mr. Schwartz's optimism. Os Guiness, *Senior Fellow of the Trinity Forum,* warns us that our best attempts to read the signs of the times are finite and fallible, so we must always be modest and open to correction.[5] There are just too many wild cards out there, and many experts, both in the realm of economics and other disciplines, are not so sanguine. They worry about the levels of debt in the system, both public in some nations, and private in others. They are concerned about the fragility of a global economic system that is now so intensely interconnected that if America sneezes economically, the rest of the world inevitably catches the flu. They worry about areas of military instability and the impact of environmental degradation.

Tom Sine, one of the world's leading Christian futurists, points out that "we are rapidly moving into a more uncertain economic future in which many of us are likely to be more vulnerable and most of us aren't prepared for a serious downturn." He believes there are two possible scenarios that are ahead of us—a long boom, but more likely, "the crashing of a slow meltdown."[6] Each would carry challenges with it for the churches, but the latter would inevitably put enormous pressure on parish, diocesan, and ministry budgets.

### Spirituality and Fiscal Health

Whichever way the economy goes, Robert Wuthnow, Princeton professor and researcher of all things religious, believes that there is a close relationship between spiritual malaise and fiscal woes—and he is not too happy about the spiritual health of the churches. His studies have led him to conclude that American churches are now standing on the brink of "an unparalleled economic crisis. It consists—as all economic crises do—of a gap between revenues and expenditures."[7] At the heart of this crisis, as far as Wuthnow is concerned, is not so much the possibility of the roof of the nation's prosperity falling in, although that could happen, but the fact that Christian people are not drawing the close connection between their spirituality and their everyday lives.

Toward the end of his analysis, Wuthnow sounds a loud warning:

> It is troubling, however, to hear how clergy talk about the future of
> the church. Those who say it will remain strong in the future base
> their arguments on the logic of necessity: Because people *need*
> spirituality, they argue, the churches will remain strong. They fail
> to recognize that growing numbers of people are looking outside
> the churches for spiritual guidance. Other pastors base their opti-
> mism on theological grounds, paying little attention to social con-
> ditions. They argue that the church will prosper because God has
> promised it would. Those who are less optimistic generally focus
> more on changing circumstances . . . What most clergy fail to rec-
> ognize are the ways in which current economic conditions in the
> churches themselves will have an impact on the future.[8]

Despite the bullish cries coming from commerce and Wall Street,
what goes up must eventually come down. In the waning days of the
last century, traders were singing the praises of the dot-com companies as the future standard bearers of the economy; early in 2000 they
fell from grace with a mighty crash—evidence of how fragile this
emerging new world really is. Furthermore, however well it is managed, and however innovative and forceful it continues to be, the U.S.
economic boom cannot go on forever. Optimists might be predicting
the Dow Jones Average with highs of 35,000–40,000, but looking at the
levels of certain investments on Wall Street pessimists are already
warning that the stock market is impossibly overvalued and that the
bubble is bursting. Meanwhile, there are regularly periods of intense
instability—made worse by greater global interconnectivity, which
means there are even more wild cards out there, variables that are
highly subject to fluctuation.

America's economic health is also profoundly influenced by the
vigor of the global economy—once again, globalization rears its head!
Just as worldwide economic markets have all started to merge, meaning
that a person can trade twenty-four hours a day seven days a week if he
or she really wanted to, so the planet's economy has become a single
whole with regional strengths, weaknesses, and characteristics that inevitably ricochet against one another. It only requires, say, China to attempt an all-out assault on Taiwan, and not only would the world's
chip-making capacity be severely damaged because Taiwan is a major
producer and crucial to the microchip industry, but such an act of vio-
lence would overnight alter all our economic prospects.[9]

Many parishes and judicatories are far from ready for the cold winds that will eventually blow, whether the economy starts shivering in six months or six years, and whether the downturn is short or protracted. You do not need to have an MBA to figure out the economic realities and then to plot a fairly accurate course as to where these might lead us.

### Where Does the Money Come From?

One fundamental factor that makes aging churches particularly vulnerable is that they are more highly dependent on the giving of older people than virtually all other institutions within our culture—one study suggests as much as 80 percent of all giving is by those who are fifty-five and over. People who are older than the traditional retirement age are not only far more likely to be part of a church than those who are younger, but because of the era in which they were raised, they have been conditioned to philanthropic generosity in a way that later generations have not been.

The rise of a new generation of philanthropists suggests that younger generations will acquire these charitable skills, but probably not quickly enough to cover the inevitable financial shortfalls. In addition, there are proportionately fewer younger people who claim Christian faith than in the older part of the population. Even those from the younger generations who are Christian and who have been schooled in the principles of stewardship are irritated that the churches continue to ask for and receive funds in a way that suits their elders. One younger person has expressed frustration that the church is so culturally conditioned to the giving practices of the older portion of the population that they have yet even to consider seriously adopting ways of receiving gifts that resonate with those who are younger. She complained that the church, its parishes, and organizations are almost all resistant to electronic approaches to giving with which her generation are most comfortable.

Not only would it be very natural to her to organize her donations via direct debit from bank accounts, but also she would like the ability to make Web donations by clicking on the appropriate box on a particular site. The failure to think in these terms reflects the inability of the churches to recognize that the Internet is the environment in which many of their younger members are comfortable, and which could be a rich source of tithes and offerings. This was illustrated by the straight-talking Senator John McCain in his run for the Republican nomination for the presidency in 2000, who so caught the imagination of younger voters for a time that he was able to use his Web site to accumulate several million dollars in order to take on his opponent and conduct a viable and dynamic primary campaign. For instance, imagine a church credit or debit card, whereby purchases generate a small return for the church. These can mount up over time.

It is imperative that we think in new terms because those elders who have been so generous are being taken from us by time and health. You only have to sit for twenty minutes with a group of older church people and you will find them talking wistfully about those of their contemporaries who have either died or found it necessary to enter some kind of care facility. Seniors also become more cautious in their giving practices, because they are more conscious of their own financial limitations and vulnerability than most who are fifty and younger. They often live on fixed incomes, uncertain dividends from investments, and their memories of the Great Depression; all this means they are going to be a lot more prudent than those of the post-World War II generations.

Ronald E. Vallet and Charles E. Zech wrote an extremely insightful book a few years ago titled *The Mainline Church's Funding Crisis.* In it they summarized this circumstance perfectly, putting the money crunch within its demographic context:

> Individuals who are members of mainline denominations continue to make contributions to their congregations. Some give less to their congregations because they also give to parachurch organizations and/or televangelists. Others give less because of concern about abuses by some televangelists, clergy sexual misconduct, and other ethical failings. In most mainline denominations, there are fewer members to make contributions. This is related, in part, to the relative absence of the Baby Boom generation (born 1946–64) in mainline congregations. Persons born before 1946 tend to give from conviction. The average age of the members of mainline denominations is rising steadily. Members of the Baby Boom generation who are present in mainline congregations give not so much from conviction and trust of the institution as from being convinced and persuaded. Trust of the institution is diminishing.[10]

Even in the unlikely event that there is not a major financial downturn in the next few years, the changing demographics in American churches in general, and the older mainline churches in particular, are going to force fiscal issues to the forefront for most parishes, dioceses, and church organizations. Here and there we already see once-solvent Christian entities experiencing economic stress, and as uncomfortable as this reality is, such concerns will become more widespread—especially in those parishes that are slow to become mission-driven, are weak in teaching and formation, and do not major in areas of stewardship.

### The Largest Capital Transfer Ever

What puzzles me is how little interest most parishes have taken in the significant transfer of wealth that is taking place at the moment as the older generation bows out and passes its accumulated assets on to their heirs and successors. It is estimated that with the passing of the aging G.I. generation approximately $16 trillion of assets is being handed on to their heirs and successors, some of which they have earmarked for philanthropic purposes.

However, while institutions such as the Episcopal Church Foundation and the Presbyterian Church (USA) Foundation have set themselves up to enable significant gifts to pass into the hands of Christian ministry, relatively few individuals have seriously availed themselves of these services. The Presbyterians have done a much better job with their foundation, but all of us have a long way to go. While building endowment alone is not the long-term answer to the problem, it would at least provide breathing space for hard-pressed parishes, dioceses, and ministries while they regroup to confront the harsher realities of the twenty-first century.

One crumb of comfort from this situation is that we are beginning to see those who recognize their vulnerability to declining dollars and numbers showing a sharpened interest in church growth, church planting, evangelism, and mission. The effort by the Episcopal Diocese of Texas, under the leadership of Bishop Claude Payne, to grow itself off a plateau of both numbers and dollars, has caught the imagination of more than forty other dioceses in the Episcopal Church, all of whom are eager to follow the Texan example.

This augers well for the future, although going to conferences and paying attention to what is going on in one corner of the country is going to require significant hard work if it is to be transplanted elsewhere. However, if the dynamic is merely to pay the bills, then it is not ultimately going to get us anywhere. After all, the church is not primarily a financial entity, though it requires and handles a lot of money—in 1999 it was estimated that offerings in the Episcopal Church exceeded over $1 billion.

Those parishes, dioceses, and church institutions that are prayerful and mission-driven must also be frugal. They must practice the teachings about Christian stewardship within the context of wholehearted discipleship and are likely to be the ones who will have the resources to steer themselves through the choppy fiscal waters that could lie ahead. People no longer give because they feel duty-bound, even those who appear to nurture a Christian commitment. But they will give sacrificially to a cause they believe in with all their heart, soul, mind, and strength. We can no longer assume that they will give generously to something that is akin to another service organization, or seems tired, boring, irrelevant and meaningless. If telethons, capital campaigns, and save the so-and-so drives can produce millions of dollars in revenue for worthy causes, the same spirit of giving can readily be tapped in support of the ministry of Christ's church.

### Finding a Variety of Ways to Pay the Bills

A further component of the changing financial picture is the need for parishes to look seriously for multiple streams of income. Just as museums and art galleries have found that they need to enter the retail business in order to keep themselves solvent, so churches and Christian bodies are likely to find themselves needing to do all sorts of creative things in order to bring in cash flow from other directions—and that means more than organizing Christmas bazaars and monster garage sales. While a steady flow of pledged gifts to God's work is vitally important, we need to be carefully looking at other ways to fund our ministries—and different methods of collecting those funds.

In addition, communicating of the substantial cost of keeping the church's business afloat is going to be even more essential than it is today. This is an era in which full disclosure is of vital importance, and people want to know where Christian bodies stand financially. This is important not only because in the wake of scandals of the nineties people do not necessarily trust Christian organizations to honor their fiduciary responsibilities, but because Boomers and Generation Xers want to know the facts—all of them.

Many churches have for years rented out their premises to schools or other groups, thus underwriting some of their overhead, but I suspect that we will need to go far beyond property rental in the future. Not only does the creative use of our buildings help with the heavy cost of maintaining them, but it also is likely to bring people over the threshold who might not otherwise go anywhere near a church—thus reducing the "shock" if they want to explore faith issues, and giving us a way in which to be friendly toward them. Such efforts require creativity and imagination, but could pay huge dividends.

Just looking at the realities, it seems to be neither good business nor mission sense to keep huge buildings warmed and/or cooled for literally an hour or two of use per week. Often I hear congregations complaining that their plant is a liability that is draining them of funds. The time has come to be imaginative, creative, and entrepreneurial, and to turn our facilities into assets rather than liabilities, although it is important that we stay within the bounds of the law.

Then we ought also to take seriously the practice of charging user fees for certain of the services that the congregation might offer. Lyle Schaller, the most experienced and best recognized American church consultant has said, "One of the most rapid-growing streams is the income derived from user fees for everything from child care to tuition to trips to meals to fees for special programs, classes, and events. These may include instruction in cardiopulmonary resuscitation or music or Bible study or concerts or income tax preparation or exercise classes or computer skills."[11]

Near the place where I grew up in England is a country house that until recently was the European headquarters of a well-known quasi-eastern religious/lifestyle group. A number of years ago they were able to purchase this grand estate and several hundred acres of grounds for a song. This splendid Victorian home once belonged to the fabulously wealthy Rothschild family, and was given by the first Lord Rothschild to one of his daughters on her marriage to an earl who later became Prime Minister of Great Britain—and whose horses were the pride of the racing fraternity!

Through good management of the user fees that they collect from those who attend their seminars and made use of their spiritual resources, the group that bought the building has been able to accumulate a significant financial reserve to advance their cause—and build their empire, which stretches far beyond self-help and Westernized Eastern belief systems. They have recently sold the building at a vast profit, and that sale has funded the modern purpose-built facility in which their headquarters is now located. While Christians may not be particularly happy with certain facets of their message, there is an awful lot we can learn from them businesswise.

While it is important that we exclude no one through their inability to pay, it is also imperative that we learn to raise money to advance ministry through the services we offer to those who could well afford them. This may be controversial in many circles, especially those who expect everything around the church to be free, but just as an American expects to pay for health care services, so also are there certain ancillary services of the church that could well become either self-funding or assist the whole congregation to underwrite some of its other expenses.

You do not need to spend too long wandering around the Internet to discover all sorts of imaginative and original approaches to funding worthy causes. Each day, for example, I can go to The Hunger Site (www.the-hungersite.com/index.html), learn an important fact about world hunger, and by my pressing a button in the middle of the screen I commit one of the site's sponsors to make a small donation to relieve famine somewhere. If I want to shop online, I can go through GreaterGood.com, purchase what I want from well-known retailers, and commit them to giving a gift to the charity of my choice from a list that is offered.

If I visit the World Vision Web Site, not only can I make a gift online to the work of this global Christian relief agency, but I can also donate to them a vehicle, stock, or go shopping for the benefit of their ministry similarly to GreaterGood.com. There are precious few mainline ministries that I am aware of that give me the same benefits. While this may not be something that most fifty-somethings like me are comfortable with, it does appeal to my adult daughters and their generation—and they are already a financial force to be reckoned with from their teens upward.

We have been trapped for too long in the "business as usual" mentality, and our attitude toward money fits into this category. We continue to assume that because the income has always appeared through traditional channels, it will continue to be the case. Anyone who keeps an eye on the levels of philanthropic giving will know that although the largest proportion of all charitable dollars still goes to churches and religious causes, little by little the balance is changing. Boomers and Generation Xers, raised with an eye to the damage we are doing to the environment, are starting to pour significant sums into environmental organizations, such as the Sierra Club and other such causes that present them with project-driven approaches in which these people believe they have some ownership and investment.

Our fiscal circumstances in the U.S.A. have international implications. For almost the whole of the twentieth century, it was the American churches that were the financial engine for the mission of the church around the world. As our financial pool shrinks, and we are forced to cut back, this will have an impact in many of those areas of the world where U.S. dollars have made a difference between God's work getting done and local Christians having to close shop. While this is not to say that the church's mission would collapse if there was nothing coming from this country, it would make it much more difficult for Africans, say, to proclaim Christ in an attractive manner vis-a-vis the challenge being mounted by Muslims, who are funded by petrodollars from the Arabian Peninsula.[12]

During the next ten to fifteen years I fully expect the issue of dollars and cents to rise higher and higher up the agenda of most Christian bodies. It is likely that we will see more and more Christian bodies being forced to make difficult decisions as the dollars wane. Meanwhile, those who have prepared themselves for changed circumstances and are firm in their commitment to the church's mission and biblical approaches to giving are likely to be in a position to advance while others are contracting.

✦ ✦ ✦

### To Think and Talk Over

1. Look at the financial circumstances of your congregation, the demographics that shape the membership, and ask some of the difficult questions about future potential cash flow.
2. If you were designing a stewardship course for your parish, what biblical and practical truths would you want to emphasize?
3. It has been said that the dollars are out there, they are just kept firmly in our pockets. How true is this?
4. What Christian ministries around the world do you support that could be damaged if your parish were forced to cut back on mission giving?
5. What have you and your congregation done to multiply the streams of income coming into your parish? What other sources of income do you potentially have? How creative are you being?
6. Planned giving is a key to future financial stability. Has your congregation and have you individually taken advantage of the possibilities that this offers?
7. Do you think that fear about future fiscal stability is a scare?

### Suggestions for Further Reading

Schaller, Lyle E. *Innovations in Ministry: Models for the Twenty-First Century* (Nashville, TN: Abingdon Press, 1994).

Vallet, Ronald E., and Zech, Charles E. *The Mainline Church's Funding Crisis: Issues and Possibilities* (Grand Rapids; MI, Manlius, NY: Wm. B. Eerdmans Publishing Co., and REV/Rose Publishing, 1995).

Wuthnow, Robert. *The Crisis in the Churches: Spiritual Malaise, Fiscal Woe* (NY: Oxford University Press, 1997).

### Web Sites

- I would recommend that any parish thinking seriously about developing a planned giving program should contact the Episcopal Church Foundation, whose site can be reached through the Web site of the Episcopal Church at www.dfms.org. Other mainline denominations have their own foundations that undertake similar jobs on their behalf. The Presbyterian Church of the U.S.A.'s foundation can be reached at www.fdn.pcusa.org. Details of the National Association of United Methodist Foundations can be found under "Planned Giving" at www.umc.org.

- For online shopping that is beneficial to charitable organizations go to www.GreaterGood.com, or you will find World Vision International at www.wvi.org. Another site that enables you to shop online and choose the organization you give to in the process is www.iGive.com.

- One of the most thoughtful ministries challenging the commonly held assumptions about stewardship and the management of our assets is the Ministry of Money. They have scads of excellent resources and run some of the most challenging conferences, retreats, and pilgrimages of reverse mission. Their Web site, www.ministryofmoney.org, is well worth a visit—but if you get involved be prepared to be challenged to the very roots of your being so that you are never the same again!

- Another site that is worth a visit is www.newtithing.org. Set up by Claude Rosenberg, a retired West Coast financier, it is designed to show people how they can double or triple their giving to causes of their choice in creative and exciting ways—and it is not just designed to talk to the wealthy, but ordinary folks like most of those reading this book.

# TREND FIVE
# Radically Changing Demographics

*Religious researchers are already predicting that sixty per-
cent of the congregations now in existence will be closed by
2050. Will your congregation be among this number? You
will have to make decisions about this now—or you will be
too far behind the starting line to survive the changes that
are already pressing in upon the church, whether you know
it or not.*[1]
Norman Shawchuck and Gustave Rath, church consultants

### Wishful Statistics

It does not matter how you crunch the numbers, the future statistics for
almost all the churches in the U.S.A. do not look as good as many of us
would like to kid ourselves. Both church attendance and then the more
detailed information that is hidden within the other arrays of statistics
that are available tell some alarming stories. In the previous chapter we
were taking a careful look at the financial challenges before us: Some
are closely related to demographic factors.

As we have seen already, there is increasing evidence that the church
attendance statistics that have been accepted for many years, suggesting
roughly a 35–45 percent attendance rate each week by Americans,
might be exaggerated.[2] During the many years that I have traveled
around this continent, my observations have led me to conclude that
there are a growing numbers of areas in the U.S.A. and Canada where
the churched population now matches that in many parts of Europe—

something that would have been unthinkable when I moved here from England a quarter century ago.

My first landfall in the United States in the mid-seventies was Massachusetts, even then hardly one of the most religiously observant areas of the country. My initial impression on arriving here was how much more religious Americans where than their British counterparts. On my most recent trips to New England it has seemed clear that, if anything, in certain communities in states like Vermont, Massachusetts, and New Hampshire, church attendance lags behind the practice of inhabitants of the village where my brother lives in the south of England.

### The Missing Generations and Leadership

Then, as you begin to scrutinize the "small print" in the data available to us, two diametrically opposed trends stand out. On the one hand, the percentage of younger people involved in church life is going down with each passing generation, and on the other hand, this generation is experiencing a quickening of spiritual interest. The accumulating evidence for this is indisputable. A recent report from Canada, for example, suggests that the proportion of fifteen to twenty-four-year-olds who worship in Christian churches there is hovering around the 12 percent mark, while a fifty-year decline in church attendance in all Canadian provinces continues unchecked. "Everyone involved agrees the churches, Protestant and Catholic, can no longer take attendance or support for granted."[3]

The mainline churches south of the forty-ninth parallel are in the same boat. Perhaps that is one reason why congregations in the historic churches tend to be older rather than younger, and until very recently they have done little either to address the enormous challenge that such a generation presents, or raise up, train, and equip younger leadership. One of the most shocking statistics that came out of the Zacchaeus Report, a comprehensive survey of the state of the Episcopal Church produced by the Episcopal Church Foundation in 1999, was that the church continues to ordain the same generation, by and large, that we were ordaining a quarter of a century ago—except they are now in their later forties rather than mid-twenties.[4] The dynamics in the other mainline denominations are somewhat similar to those in the Episcopal Church.

It is a relief to see that some mainliners have begun to address this, even to give priority to younger vocations to ordination, but until the processes that the older churches use are radically overhauled they will continue to favor the older rather than the younger aspirant, the mature over those whose youth puts them at a disadvantage when seeking to find their way through "the system." I have a friend who is a member of an Episcopal diocesan Commission on Ministry, the body that helps select candidates for ordination. He said to me recently when we were discussing this particular issue, "Let's stop dancing around how we say no to older aspirants who we do not believe the diocese should ordain. Let us just tell them it *is* an issue of age."

This failure to raise up new young leadership will require of the Episcopal Church, and other mainline denominations, a crash course in identifying, nurturing, training, and placing new leadership. Some projections that have developed out of my recent research suggest that the Episcopal Church will be needing somewhere in the region of 5,000–6,000 new priests, most of them at the younger end of the spectrum, during the next fifteen years. Even if this figure is inflated, the number of young clergy required presents not just a colossal challenge, but an extraordinary opportunity.

Our circumstances in the Episcopal Church have been intensified by a decision made by the church's pension fund to allow clergy with thirty years of service under their belts to retire with full benefits after they reach the age of fifty-five. A steady flow of clergy now in their late fifties or early sixties, and who have their thirty years, have decided to take their money and explore options other than parish ministry. This means that some dioceses are already facing longer and longer vacancies in parishes because there are just not enough, "junior" priests around to fill those jobs.

These days, if you are looking for a pastor for an Episcopal congregation who is fresh out of seminary, he or she is more likely to be around the age of forty-five to fifty, and will probably be far less mobile than the handful of their younger counterparts. And they will not be around for so long either. We can probably estimate that 60 to 75 percent of the present Episcopal clergy force will retire by 2015.

As we look at the sort of clergy we need to lead the church in this new millennium, it is important that we find men and women who are self-starters and have entrepreneurial skills. Because of the processes and priorities of the path toward ordination, in the last thirty years the church has sought those who are primarily pastorally oriented, women and men who are not likely to make too many unfortunate waves. We need far fewer traditional professional clergy and many more missionary pastors who can lead the process of transformation.

A few years ago, in an interview with *Christianity Today*, Bishop Bill Frey, who had at that time just stepped down as president of Trinity Episcopal School for Ministry, said, "I think the church needs to recruit the brightest and the best, rather than just passively receive those people who volunteer for ministry—challenge pastors and youth group leaders to mentor people who look like future CEOs. Jesus didn't sit dangling his feet in the Jordan River hoping a few people would come along. He recruited."[5] At this juncture in history we desperately need to be identifying and recruiting church planters and creative change agents who are capable of leading back to life moribund parishes, or to reinvigorate those that have settled for a survival mode of operation.

Having served on a Commission on Ministry for a number of years, I have reached the conclusion that there has to be a better way of selecting tomorrow's leaders. The process we have in place in so many judicatories seems designed to cull the best from the pack and declare them unfit for leadership. Although I am not sure that North American Anglicans either could or would be comfortable going back to the days when the bishop would take aside a likely young person and say, "I'm sending you off to seminary to be a priest," there are real flaws in the system we now use. This committee approach to selection is an outmoded process designed to cull out would be "troublemakers," a practice that guarantees we will miss the majority of those with the sort of skills necessary for twenty-first century-leadership. We should create what I would call the "Brightest and Best" movement. Its sole purpose would be to identify, nurture, and prepare for leadership the very best of our people.[6]

### The Missing Generations and Youth Ministry

In addition to our failure to raise up young leadership, for too long we have held onto outdated notions of youth ministry. Taking our cue from the 1960s and 1970s the view has prevailed that we should let them go away and sow their wild oats, and they will be back as they get older. This mindset has provided an excuse in many mainline congregations for youth ministry to be allowed to slide. The presupposition upon which such an attitude is based is just plain wrong! The evidence is in and is overwhelming that treated in this way the young will *never* come back. There are just too many other alternative choices in such a pluralistic world—besides as many as 80 percent of all adult Christians made their initial commitment to Jesus Christ before they reached their twentieth birthday.

Yes, a few Baby Boomers did come back to church once they grew up, but while estimates vary wildly about those who left forever, we probably lost about 40 percent of that generation—or around thirty million people. The next two generations have grown up in a culture that is far less favorably disposed toward the churches. Even if it is less overtly secular, so many of them have no memory of churchgoing respectability, neither are they inclined to trust such an institution even if they are intrigued by certain aspects of its spirituality.

Dieter and Valerie Zander, a gifted pair of nondenominational church planters in San Francisco, talking about the challenge of ministry among the young, describe the rising generation as "ignostics." The young, they assert, do not present the churches with a generational challenge so much as a philosophical challenge. They are thoroughly Postmodern in their worldviews, with the result that they say, "My view of the world, truth, and spirituality is significantly different from your view of the world." The gap between the churches and the young is widening as churches' Modern, Enlightenment-shaped approach to ministry speaks to a smaller and smaller percentage of people.

The Zanders go on to say that "these (younger) people have not even rejected God so much as ignored him. Others have rejected a god who is a mere caricature of the living God . . . Many Postmodern people do not have any residual understanding of the triune God and his story. To assume that they do is deadly to anyone who wants to communicate with them."[7]

Yet despite these added complexities, as we have already seen, the evidence overwhelmingly suggests that it is while people are in their teens and twenties that they are most open to respond to the Gospel. Every ounce of creativity, dollar, and volunteer hour that is invested in the young is going to pay far greater dividends than we imagine. Our tendency is to put resources elsewhere, and then wonder where the young are. If we refuse to learn this lesson and fail to invest wisely, we have only ourselves to blame for the consequences. In those places where youth ministry is being taken seriously, and Christian education is given the highest priority and is presented in a manner that is both attractive and excellent, young families by the score are finding their way into congregations—regardless of the denominational label on the church sign.

My elder daughter, Olivia, now in her late twenties, dropped out of church life as a teenager. Naturally, this set her mother and I praying. She had been well grounded in the faith and had been educated in a church-sponsored school, but she needed space from being a preacher's kid. Today she and her husband, Joe, both former Episco-palians, have been re-evangelized by a lively Presbyterian congregation in the city where they used to lived, and my son-in-law is now in sem-inary training for leadership in the life of that church. Of course, we are delighted that they are part of such a supportive church, although disappointed that virtually every Episcopal church in the city where they used to live is so committed to other issues that it seems to have little concern for twenty-somethings who are anxious about for the health of their souls. Not only is excellent Christian education and youth ministry necessary, but so is the follow-through of a congenial environment for younger adults.

### Interdenominational Youth and Campus Ministries

Although in the Episcopal Church there are dioceses like South Car-olina that have invested heavily in youth ministry and are seeing the dividends after a number of years pursuing this policy, congregations that take seriously the formation of the young tend to be the exception rather than the rule in the older denominations. Some of the best youth and college ministry today is being done by folks like Young Life, Cam-pus Life, InterVarsity Christian Fellowship, and the Fellowship of Christian Athletes, and despite the fact that disproportionate numbers of mainline Christians are in the leadership of some of these ministries, a large proportion of members of those denominations tend to get very sniffy about such organizations. Meanwhile many of our church-spon-sored high school and college campus efforts are mostly down some-where on the depressing to lifeless end of the spectrum.

Having mentioned my elder daughter let me balance things out by talking of Lindy, my younger daughter, who is at medical school. Like her sister, she attended the same excellent Episcopal school, but she was still a student there when the ministry of Young Life was launched on that high school campus. Through the relational nurture of Young Life she made her personal commitment of faith in Christ, and was lovingly cultivated and cared for by a faithful volunteer, a college student, dur-ing her early believing.

She attended an Episcopal church as an undergraduate and is now well into medical school training. Today she is part of yet another Epis-copal congregation, and it has been evangelical campus groups that have played the largest role in helping as she has continued to grow in the faith. It pleases me that she has a deepening spiritual life focused on

Jesus Christ, but when I have mentioned the sources of her support to some of my clergy friends, they have turned up their noses that any thinking person could affiliate and benefit from such groups. Thus we come face-to-face with our own prejudices.

Twenty years ago, Richard G. Hutchinson wrote, "The generation . . . produced in mainline churches with their attention fixed on social change . . . lacks that rooting in a deep faith."[8] Little has changed. Despite their many shortcomings, about which Christians from the historic Protestant churches of America are constantly whining, evangelical churches and parachurch organizations are still doing a better job at forming the young in Christ and providing deep roots for their faith. If we are not prepared to learn lessons from them and cooperate with them, we do not deserve to stay in business.

In our denomination, at least, it seems we have been much more intent on making "little Episcopalians" rather than bringing along "young Christians." Whatever their theological and ecclesiastical biases, Episcopalians are proud of their church—and I share this joy in our tradition. We must beware of such pride because it tends to skew our perceptions of reality, with the result that we tend to end up focusing on irrelevant minutiae—majoring in the minors, as it were. It is far more important that young people be given every opportunity to encounter Jesus Christ in a vibrant way, and be formed by the substance of the Gospel message as found in Scripture, than be able to tell you what the liturgical colors are for the church's year.

As young people hassle with the extraordinary and complex issues that confront them in the process of coming-of-age in our society, churchiness, which lost its appeal years ago, no longer cuts the ice. Church is like being far from home in a foreign land, and possibly it even appears to be a hostile environment. Given these circumstances, denominational identity should take a backseat to Christian unity.

We need to discover different ways of looking at our denominational families. Denominations are entities that preserve many important facets of our tradition, but there needs to be a rethinking of how denominations set the agenda or drive the curriculum, for the truth is that the coming generation does not prioritize denominational distinctiveness over Christian inclusiveness. These structures and institutions are the stand upon which the lamp of the Gospel is placed, the depository of our tradition, but they are not the Gospel itself. Furthermore, the sun has started to set on much of what denominations have stood for in the past one hundred years—and woe betide us if we overlook this fact.

## Ethnic, Household, and Demographic Diversity

While we need to devote a tremendous amount more attention to the demographics of age, we also need to be aware of the way demographics are shifting elsewhere. There is no such thing as the "average" Episcopal or mainline congregation, but in most places around the country our churches have traditionally catered to white, middle-class, and generally middle-aged people, the majority of whom are living in nuclear families.

Not only do many of our structures make it difficult for the single, the single again, and those who just do not fit, to be part of our life together, but we are oblivious to the needs of an American population that is still growing faster than the populations of virtually every other developed nation, while rapidly diversifying ethnically. The U.S. Census Bureau expects the American population to have more than doubled by 2100, with 571 million people living here as opposed to the 275 million now. The Associated Press summarizes the Census findings as follows:

The median age in 2100 is expected to be 40.3, compared to the current 35.8. Median means half of all Americans will be older than that and half younger.

The Hispanic population is expected to triple from 31.4 million in 1999 to 98.2 million in 2050. Hispanics could become the nation's largest minority group with their percentage rising from 12 percent in 1999 to 24 percent in 2050. The Asian and Pacific Islander population, meanwhile, would more than triple, from 10.9 million in 1999 to 37.6 million in 2050. Its percentage of the total population would rise from 4 percent now to 9 percent in 2050.

According to the projections, the non-Hispanic White and African-American populations would increase more slowly than the other groups. The non-Hispanic White population would rise from 196.1 million in 1999 to 213.0 million in 2050, a 9 percent increase. Its share of the total population would decline, however, from 72 percent in 1999 to 53 percent in 2050.

The black population would rise from 34.9 million in 1999 to 59.2 million in 2050, a 70 percent increase; under this projection, the black share of the total population would increase slightly, from 13 percent to 15 percent.

The projections for racial and ethnic groups are given only through 2050 because the figures are considered less reliable for the latter parts of the century. Between 1999 and 2050, the total number of foreign-born would more than double, increasing from 26.0 million to 53.8 million. The proportion of the nation's population that is foreign-born would rise from 10 percent in 1999 to 13 percent in 2050.[9]

However accurate these projections are, they shout from the house-tops that a very different America is being born from the one that we have been used to—and the characteristics of this emerging America are something that our church has yet to come to terms with, let alone address. The burgeoning Millennial generation—those born since the early 1980s—are the most ethnically diverse American generation ever, tangible evidence of the "browning" of America. We are still living as if this land were still predominantly white, Protestant, and Anglo-Saxon.

I can illustrate how fast the U.S.A. is changing from what has been happening in middle Tennessee where we have lived during the last fifteen years of the old century, although something similar is occurring in many other parts of the country. When my family and I moved to Tennessee in the mid-eighties, the Episcopal churches were overwhelmingly racially and socially monochrome. There were a few African-Americans, but the vast majority of Episcopalians were (and are) of white Anglo-Saxon and Celtic lineage. But middle Tennessee is no longer "hick" or "red neck" country, and is fast becoming as cosmopolitan a community as Atlanta, Dallas, Seattle, or Boston.

There are now growing numbers of Sudanese, Nigerians, Ugandans, and other Africans, all from Anglican backgrounds, joining Tennessee's Episcopal parishes, and we don't know how to reach out to them and enfold them. Such diversity reflects the growth of these ethnic groups in this fast-altering region. Before 1992 there were hardly any Sudanese here; now that figure is climbing beyond 3,000 in the Greater Nashville area, and more arrive every week. The same is true of a whole range of other ethnic groups from all over the world—each bringing with them an array of religious or non-religious commitments that are shaking the foundations of this Bible Belt region.

The majority of Episcopal congregations are sticking to the older way of doing things and have tended to close their eyes to the challenge being presented by growing Korean-, Spanish-speaking, and other ethnic populations. Rutherford, the county in which I live, was a quiet haven in the rural South when we came to Tennessee fifteen years ago. Now there are children speaking forty-six native tongues in the public schools—and while there is no synagogue, we do have a Buddhist temple and a growing Muslim community!

The world has come to Tennessee, but Christians in Tennessee are still so puzzled about how to cope with it that they tend to leave it alone and stick to the "tried-and-true" way of being church. The only problem is that the "tried-and-true" does not hold much water any longer with the majority of the population either. Let me hasten to add that I am not "picking" on Tennessee Christians as being less sensitive or more dense than their compatriots elsewhere—our attitudes here are typical of mainline Christians from coast-to-coast in these United States.

Caucasian Americans, whether they express it this way or not, tend to see this variegating of our nation as threatening—and certainly it means that many of our cultural presuppositions are going to be forced to change. However, we need to start thinking differently—this array of demographic changes is an extraordinary opportunity for mission and ministry. What is important is that we grasp what is going on around us so that we know where and how to focus our prayers and efforts.

### How Do We Respond?

It is vital that we work hard to understand the changing demographics of our own neighborhoods—and then set about learning how to be missionary within this setting. It is crucial that our clergy and lay leadership learn to read and understand local, regional, and national demographic trends—only then will they know how to strategize. As we study the figures, thereby discovering what is going on, we will be enabled to see the vast openings that will help us become missionaries to our own little world. Such work is no longer a luxury, but an overwhelming necessity.

One parish I know did something like this. They concluded that 90,000 members live within what they considered their natural geographical "catchment" area, at least thirty percent of whom are totally unchurched. They then looked at themselves and the diversity of people living in that area, and reckoned they had a fighting chance with 3–4 percent of the population—and they are now creating strategies to seek ways to reach out to them with the Good News of Jesus Christ.

If congregations continue to ignore such demographic realities, and think only in terms of corralling that shrinking and aging band of practicing Episcopalians, Presbyterians, or Methodists who might move into their locality, then they have probably jeopardized all chances of a future. The evidence is that 60–70 percent of all American congregations now in existence are likely to go out of business in the next forty to fifty years. Given present trends, Episcopal and other mainline churches will make up a disproportionate number of those soon-to-be extinct parishes.

✦ ✦ ✦

### *To Think and Talk Over*

1. Why do you think it is that people may not tell the truth to pollsters about their churchgoing? What do you think this says about their attitude toward the health of their souls?
2. If you are under the age of thirty, what keeps you from being part of your present parish? If you are under thirty, what irritates you about the style of the parish?
3. What do you think it is about interdenominational youth and campus ministries that puts so many Episcopalians and other mainlines off?
4. Why do we seem determined to make little Episcopalians, Presbyterians, etc., rather than followers of Christ?
5. How have the ethnic and social demographics of your neighborhood altered in the last twenty years?
6. What have you done to reach out to the unchurched in your area?

### *Suggestions for Further Reading*

Barna, George. *Generation Next—What You Need to Know about Today's Youth* (Ventura, CA: Regal Books, 1995).

Beaudoin, Tom. *Virtual Faith—The Irreverent Spiritual Quest of Generation X* (Jossey-Bass, San Francisco, 1998).

Cimino, Richard P. *Against the Stream—The Adoption of Traditional Christian Faiths by Young People* (Lanham: University Press of America, 1997).

Easum, William M. *Sacred Cows Make Gourmet Burgers* (Nashville, TN: Abingdon Press, 1995).

Howe, Neil, & Strauss, William. *Millennials Rising* (New York: Vintage Press, 2000).

Nash, Robert N., Jr. *An 8-Track Church in a CD World* (Macon, Georgia: Smyth and Helwys, Macon, 1997).

Reeves, Thomas C. *The Empty Church* (New York: Free Press, 1996).
Regele, Mike. *Death of the Church* (Grand Rapids, MI: Zondervan, 1995).
Roxburgh, Alan J. *The Missionary Congregation, Leadership, and Liminality* (Valley Forge, PA: Trinity Press International, 1997).

***Web Sites***

- There is a lot of helpful information available at the Web site of Methodist church consultant Bill Easum and his Canadian colleague Tom Bandy. The address is www.easumbandy.com.
- The place to go to get the statistics and to put them into perspective on a global scale is www.gem-werc.org, the Web site of the World Evangelization Research Center. One of the Founders of the Center was the Reverend Dr. David B. Barrett, an Anglican priest who has given much thought and analysis to statistics and their meaning.
- Graeme Codrington is a South African Generation Xer, and a fine youth minister. His online youth ministry publication, *The Edge,* is well worth visiting and subscribing to. His Web site address is: *The Edge, Journal of Cutting Edge Youth Ministry* http://move.to/theedge.
- There is a great deal of good material about high school campus ministry at www.younglife.org, the Web site of Young Life, an interdenominational ministry to teenagers in high school.
- Among the various youth ministry sites put up by Episcopalians, it is worth visiting the Rock the World Youth Mission Alliance site at www.episcopalian.org.

# TREND SIX
# The Fast Approaching Gray Wave

*As American society becomes more complex, more impli-*
*cated in other societies, the odds for future reinventions of*
*the nationstate get longer, especially as an aging population*
*puts additional pressure on traditional institutions. By*
*2025, America's population will be as old as Florida's is now:*
*one in five persons will be over sixty-five. By 2040, the num-*
*ber of Social Security beneficiaries will double.*[1]
    Robert D. Kaplan, writer and traveler

### The Coming Age Wave

With each passing year, America is getting older. Unlike Japan and several European countries, both the highly developed English-speaking
nations of North America have a relatively low median age—due in
large part to continued immigration of younger people from the Latin
and Asian worlds that we noted in the previous trend. Yet even despite
this, and the fact that the Millennials are even more numerous than
Boomers, America is getting older.

Countries like Italy, Spain, Germany, Russia, and Ukraine, with
birth rates that are lower than replacement and which may even have a
net outflow of emigrants, are watching the average age of their population skyrocket, while their numbers are declining. Ukraine, for example, appears to be almost too scared to carry out a long overdue census
because it is frightened it will discover a huge drop in population num-
bering several millions. Statisticians predict that, even if America's population continues to rise, as is projected, the population of developed

countries as diverse as Holland and Japan are likely to decline. No one is quite sure what the long-term implications of such a reversal will be.

A question for which there seems to be no final answer right now is: "Why have those living in the developed world 'given up' having babies?" While part of the answer to this conundrum could be the consequences of the changing role of women, and then the high costs of raising and educating children in the West, there is much more to it than just that. Another guess is that having been warned during the last decades of the previous century that overpopulation is going to be a major scourge as the third millennium begins, couples are now heeding this message. Then those who live in the former Communist world are so demoralized that many have the gravest misgivings about bringing children into such a decimated society. Whatever the reasons for lower birthrates, when put alongside the baby boom following World War II, they have created lopsided demographics.

In the U.S.A., even despite a continuing significant population flow of younger people from all over the world, our population is graying quickly, due to continuing relatively low birthrates, increased life expectancy, and the aging of the earliest cohorts of Baby Boomers. Within twenty-five years it looks likely that one in four Americans will be over retirement age, although it is also possible that many will continue working at least on a part-time basis well into their seventies.

> Beginning just after the year 2000, the first wave of 80 million Baby Boomers will reach their late fifties and begin transforming America into a place where, for the first time ever, there will be more older adults than children and youth. By 2030, the number of older adults will have doubled again, to 70 million. Between a fifth and a quarter of the country will consist of these senior citizens, a transformation that has inspired some experts to talk about the "Floridization of America." Yet, if anything, this characterization understates the change: A "mere" 19 percent of Florida's population today is over sixty-five.[2]

The twentieth century saw the condition of the elder population change radically. No longer is Grandma likely to be a penurious old lady who is malnourished, unhealthy, badly clothed, and living in squalor—or utterly dependent for her security on family charity. Today's elderly are, by and large, healthy and well looked after, and many are to be found swarming across the countryside "spending their children's inheritance" well into their seventies and eighties. America's postwar prosperity has been good to them. One need only to look at the extraordinary power of the American Association of Retired Persons (AARP) to see the influence that voting elders now wield, and the manner in which politicians, hungry for their support at the polls, pander to senior citizens.

Yet, retirement may not be the same for the next couple of generations of the elderly. It seems unlikely that the country will be able to afford to lavish the same care on those of us who are a little younger when we reach that point in life because there are so many of us and our life expectancy is so much longer. While the goodness-knows-how-many Boomers are already saying that they are not going to buy into the retirement equals leisure and self-indulgence mindset of those who have gone before them, whichever way you slice it they are going to put a strain on the system. Even if, as they indicate, a significant proportion on reaching the traditional retirement age of sixty-five decide to stay in the workforce for a few more years, the remainder are going to put a colossal burden on the economy, on health care provision, and just about everything else related to care in one's declining years.

I have watched for years as elders have sashayed into hotels, restaurants, and airlines, and been given special deals and perks. For a while I thought, "My time will come." I am not so sure now. Given the sheer volume of Boomers, it seems unlikely to me that those of us born in the twenty years following World War II will be getting many of the senior benefits that get handed out to today's elderly. If anything, an increasingly frugal culture could not begin the process of paring them back.

Furthermore, Boomers have tended to be spenders rather than savers. Although it is true that some Boomers have been thrifty, or have made a fortune on escalating residential property values or the burgeoning markets of the 1990s, many more are in debt to their eyeballs. There are many reasons for this. They may have been overly charmed by the power of easy credit, or have overspent on housing, or, perhaps they have been forced to deplete their resources providing a college education for their children. This latter is a gigantic burden on middle-class people, with the price tag on a four-year college education likely to rise to $300,000 in the next twenty years.

Some analysts say there is nothing to worry about because increased life spans make it more attractive for older people to continue working well into their "retirement" years, and therefore accumulate the kind of resources that will cushion their declining years. While it will certainly happen, and it will ease the demographic burden, it is still unlikely to take all the pressure off systems that have been consistently underfunded. While it is likely that the next generation of retirees will be more active than passive in their so-called retirement, most of the positive arguments that lengthening life expectancy will minimize the stress on the economy and systems of care are unconvincing. This will be especially the case if we see a significant tightening in the world economy.

### Globalization and Aging

This seesaw ride involving the positive benefit of longer life spans and the negative cost of living so long illustrates the push-me, pull-me life of the global village. Global factors are bound to have a profound impact in the future, right down to some of the most intimate details of our daily lives. Our prosperity is dependent on how the global economy develops during the next decade, which will significantly shape the sort of lives that many of us will have as we move into old age.

As I noted earlier, Tom Sine, the leading Christian futurist, posits two scenarios for the future. The first is a worldwide economic boom that will be so all-consuming that it is likely to devour the time and energy of those who might be available to provide some care for the elderly, and the second and more ominous one is a slow fiscal meltdown. The latter is likely to drain the funds, both private and public, that we might presently be depending upon to ensure our security for old age.[3]

There are all sorts of unanswered questions related to the rapid graying of our population. William Knoke asks, "With so many economically inactive groups (of older people), who will doctor our elderly and run our retirement homes, design our buildings and sweep our streets, pilot our jets and repair our cars? Who will support the swelling ranks of pensioned retirees? In the rich countries, instead of population growth, population *aging* will be the demographic nemesis of the early twenty-first century."[4]

The only answer that Knoke can come up with to this series of vital questions is that we do not have any other option than to open our doors to more and more younger immigrants. This will not only feed the diversification trends that we noticed in the previous chapter, but could very well exacerbate racial tensions and could aggravate new rounds of xenophobia on the part of groups that feel the most threatened by the multiplication of new arrivals. The truth is that we in America already depend upon immigration; in the years to come this will be doubly so, and our immigration laws will have to adjust to this reality.

The need for a different approach to immigration will be necessary because of the explosive growth of the population to the south of us.

The Border Patrol is having enough trouble policing the American border right now; in years to come it is likely to be even more difficult to keep illegal aliens out. Eager men, women, and children in the Global South are able to watch the lifestyle of the rich West every day on television. It is only natural for them to yearn to share it—no matter the cost. Western Europe is facing the same pressures as the U.S.A. and Canada, but in their case aliens come from Africa, Eastern Europe, and parts of Asia.

### Battered Family Systems

But the demographics have another twist. The early twenty-first century is going to have to deal with the consequences of the divorce epidemic that spread like wildfire from the 1960s onward. While some have managed to stabilize their personal lives, the outcome is that there are larger numbers than ever before who are now between forty and sixty who have, and there is no gentle way to put it, made shipwreck of many of their personal relationships. Meanwhile, others have explored a whole variety of unconventional lifestyle options. The end product is a hotchpotch of multiple marriages, spliced families, blended families, atomized families, nontraditional families, same-sex households, and much more. As the evidence accumulates, one thing that is becoming clear is that experimental lifestyles are not so stable; neither are they likely to have the staying power of more traditional family structures.

All this would suggest that we are heading into a period when a critical proportion of the population will be made up of lonely older people who have precious few blood relatives with whom to share their later years, nor have anyone to take care of them as their physical well-being declines. If the modern industrial world put pressure on relationships, the Postmodern world is one that has so gloried the individual and individuality that personal relationships have often imploded, leaving in their wake both alienation and loneliness. It would appear that the practice of a me-first lifestyle almost inevitably leads to an only-me concluding chapter of life.

Could it be that we are going to see a new and alarming array of lifestyle and relationship issues in the years ahead as a result of the battering that traditional family systems have received? It seems fair to think that more elders will be working into what previous generations considered prime retirement years just because this will be the only setting in which they can relate meaningfully with people. Their presence, and the presence of those elders who work because they choose to, could bring all sorts of pressures into the workplace. We could also find elders seeking intimacy in new kinds of relationships, some of which will be as impermanent and unsatisfactory as those they have pursued in their earlier lives.

Projecting the implication of present realities into the future, coupled with the continued likelihood that medical advances will prolong already lengthened lives, means that we will soon be scrambling to find ways to give support to the elderly. We are reaching a point where social, psychological, and economic bills are going to come due for the willful lives so many have lived. Neither society at large nor the churches will be able to side-step these realities, which means that we will face a crisis if we do not start working hard now to reinvent our later years.

Marc Freedman has been studying and working to change the nature of what he calls "the third age" for a number of years. While he accepts there is much that remains to be done, he does believe that there is an "impulse toward a new kind of later life—one that is a 'new beginning.'" He goes on to say that there is a "growing awareness among Americans that the third age is no longer a brief intermezzo between midlife and drastic decline." This "is fueling a re-examination and redefinition among many of what it means to grow old."[5]

The rising generation of senior citizens is less likely to relocate southward to warmer climates and segregated communities like Sun City, Arizona. More and more are wanting to do something constructive with their later years, and couples like Jimmy and Rosalyn Carter have provided a model of what it means to grow old not only gracefully, but actively and making a useful contribution to society. This period of our lives, the Carters tell us, is not the end but another new beginning.

### The Challenge to the Churches

Marc Freedman's book *Prime Time: How Baby Boomers Will Revolutionize Retirement and Transform America* is a perceptive and far-reaching study of aging and retirement that is filled with exciting examples of what older Americans are doing and might do in the future. He has researched and visited all sorts of encouraging programs and seeds of ideas, but apart from a brief reference to Habitat for Humanity, he says absolutely nothing about the religious community as it faces this challenge. Either this is because he is a secular person who did not look very hard, or it is because there is a lack of creativity in the churches.

The truth is that as America ages, more than just physical and psychological care will be needed. I suspect that churches (and other religious groupings) are going to be hard-pressed to help them address their spiritual needs—needs that will be intensified by the aloneness that so many are likely to experience. Boomers are a generation that has played around with things spiritual. Vast numbers of them manage to be both brashly materialistic, while maintaining an intense curiosity about the unseen world and eager to find meaning in their lives. The weaknesses of their individualistic spiritualities are likely to show up when they are isolated and in need of someone else's help.

Given all the realities spelled out above, it seems unlikely that the so-called sunset years are going to be particularly golden for a significant proportion of the Boomer generation. I have these depressing visions of them continuing to fight the aging process while sitting before their interactive digital televisions-cum-computers, chatting on the Net, or using new technologies to play virtual reality games that pretend youth and sexual virility. Such lives will be directionless and without the spiritual sustenance that will help them come to terms with life's greatest journey into eternity. They will certainly be aware of their dilemma, and might possibly look for something more meaningful and satisfying.

Yet, as sad as all this sounds, this is an extraordinary opportunity for the congregations who have eyes to see. If they work until they are sixty-five, the first Boomers will be preparing to leave the workforce in 2011. Some are already planning to retire sooner, and indeed, a few have started slowing down and are restructuring their lives around pleasure and avocations. After that there will be wave after wave of white-hairs who were young in the sixties and seventies, former conformists and counterculture types, veterans and antiwar activists, who will be altering the face of society as they have at every other stage of their existence. It is vital for the churches to develop strategies to deal with the challenges of this age wave—and the process needs to be started *now*.

### A Christian Elder Corps

For those who are believers, we need to think seriously about developing some kind of Christian elder corps that will take the resources and energies of the elderly and retirees and give them avenues where their skills and insights can be valued. This is unlikely to be a generation of elders who are content merely to sit in the church office answering the phone, stuffing envelopes, or doing the twenty-first century equivalent of licking stamps. They will want to be involved in something more significant.

As I have traveled around the world, I have run across older "retired" Christians doing some wonderful things for God. They are exciting and excited people. Some are putting to use the talents and wisdom accumulated during a well-lived life, while others are exploring other avenues of service—avenues that are keeping them alert, active, and extremely interesting. Retirement, for these people, means rejuvenation rather than atrophy.

However, one of the tragedies is the tendency of so many older Christian men and women, who have not been offered any alternatives, to turn their lives into one long round of self-indulgence. There should be more to this chapter of life than trying to shoot one's own age in golf! While there is nothing wrong with enjoying some of the fruits of seniority, these are folks for whom sports, travel, managing their portfolios, or puttering about doing piffling little jobs around the church fill the hours, but bring little satisfaction. A number of recent retirees who found the pleasure-oriented lifestyle cloying have begun to talk of this period of their lives as "The Give Back Years," and to act accordingly. These individuals are not content merely to harvest the fruit of their earlier success, but they want to contribute in some tangible way to the well-being of the human race.

Boomers are part of a generation that has always thought big. It should not be beyond our wit and wisdom to create Christian causes that will catch their imaginations, absorb their creativity, give them ownership of a mind-stretching opportunity, and thereby advance the Kingdom of our God. If they could be successful before retirement, why should they suddenly lose their value after their final day on the job and in the traditional workforce? And if their lives have lacked the successes for which they strove when younger, perhaps in retirement they will discover something that makes sense of their years and experience.

Given that medical advances and improved lifestyles mean that life spans have the potential to continue to lengthen, there is no reason why someone who has been a teacher, banker, cab driver, farmer, or beautician should not in old age use the increasing number of opportunities to benefit the church and themselves. They could, for example, use the Internet to gain a fine theological education.[6] Not only would this keep them alert and active, but it would equip them for all sorts of opportunities for Christian service that are there lined up in front of them.

There is no reason why a healthy older person should not be dispatched to work in the development of a Christian organization in a troubled country like Indonesia, or to teach in a Christian school in Central America or Africa. On a sweltering early morning in a Latin

American city some years ago, I sat drinking coffee and chatting with a couple whose whole life had been devoted to education. The church in that country could never afford the skills and insights that they brought with them in a month of Sundays, but here they were giving back to God something from the riches that their own lives had accumulated. There are myriad long- and short-term opportunities like this just waiting to be taken up.

Elder Christians who are properly trained and equipped might be able to have a profound impact in many settings, whether it be the challenge of the inner cities or by pastoring their peers. These people could very well turn the tide of the battered family syndrome. In the rush and tumble world in which we live, what elders have is more time to give to relationships. As everything from friends to foster grandparents, they are in the position to mentor and impart their wisdom to the rising generation of young people.

> Given their relative good health, financial security, mobility, and skill levels, America's senior adults have the potential to become the most effective workforce of volunteers in human history. Many of these seniors may have spent their younger years focused upon material gain and hedonistic self-indulgence; a number of them now are searching for deeper and more profound meaning in life. They are interested in useful and worthwhile endeavors in which to invest themselves, and, properly motivated, they are willing to volunteer their time, talents, and resources.[7]

Even when it is not possible for older people to take on something big, the small but important things around the church can be given much deeper meaning, especially if they are allied with a life of prayer and devotion. There is no reason why a parish should not become the focal point of intentional communities of older Christians, married, widowed, and single, who serve in unsung ways for a number of hours most days of the week, but also are committed to a regular routine of prayer and worship. One of the great gifts that senior Christians have to give is the time and the ability to pray and intercede. Maybe the models for such ministry by elders are the prophet Simeon and the prophetess Anna, whom we meet in the early chapters of St. Luke's Gospel.[8]

As greater and greater pressure is put on parish budgets by the cost of employing clergy and even minimal support staff, many parishes have just the right people in their midst who could pick up some of the slack—and more. These faithful older parishioners do not need to earn divinity degrees to be able to make a difference, although theological education could be a lot more creative in providing resources for them to fulfill their tasks and callings.

Some years ago I stayed with an elderly couple in Florida who were lively, active, and creative, and whose vision for their parish far outreached the vision of their rector! In their own quiet and unthreatening way, they were the ones who were nudging him along, rather than the other way round. I had the impression that it was their fifty-something priest who had taken premature retirement in Florida, while despite questionable health, this pair were the ones who saw old age as a fresh opportunity to serve God and their fellow human beings in new ways. Not only did the husband make sure that the parish was smoothly administered, but husband and wife together were at the forefront whenever new ministry opportunities presented themselves.

It has also been fascinating to meet a number of older Christians who, once retired and able to give thought to the eternal fate of their soul, have been transformed from non-attendees or nominal churchgoers into lively and dynamic servants of Christ. This has usually been as a result of the ministry of a parish that has taken them and their concerns seriously, and has provided for them a community in which they can explore their hearts' desires without any sense of embarrassment. Such parishes have presented Christ to them in such a way that they can finally grasp what a living faith is all about.

There is nothing more wonderful than talking to an individual whose white hair but shining eyes tell of a living, growing relationship with Jesus Christ, after a life spent giving little more than a stiff and often Episcopal "nod to God." While I was writing this chapter, I was staying for a night in the home of just such a couple—church people for whom the renewal movement, Cursillo, and the time for reflection that retirement allows had been the turning point. They admitted that their deepening Christian obedience had opened doors to serve others, and they now found themselves doing things that they had not dreamed possible just a few years earlier. Now one of their concerns was how to help their adult children and grandchildren into the freshness they have experienced in their relationship with God.

This points to another vital facet of ministry among an aging population. As we become more conscious of our own mortality, it is unusual if people do not start asking the ultimate questions. In their lifetime, some of tomorrow's oldsters may have played around with crystals and mind-altering drugs, seeking to experience life more fully. Although the benefits of all these things were supposed to be life affirming, they can provide little guidance for the ultimate journey. The quickening footsteps of death can strangely focus the mind and heart!

While the trend will continue for the majority of people to make their faith commitment during their teens and early twenties, properly approached, it seems likely that there are literally millions of seniors who, as they age, are ready to take Jesus Christ's claims a lot more seriously. Our task is to work out how graciously and caringly to reach out to them and scratch them where they itch. Could it be that Jane Fonda's apparent profession of faith in Jesus Christ, whether it sticks or not, marks her out as a pioneer following a trail many others of her generation and younger will follow?[9] Now she finds herself in her sixties and asking fascinating questions about how to use the years that remain to her on this earth.

Churches could think of using their assets to prepare to minister more effectively among the elderly (possibly through a retiree). They might develop appropriate housing for them, provide the right kind of assistance to those who are determined to work until they drop, and give meaning to the lives of those who have discovered that even those pleasurable pursuits that they dreamed about for so many years when anchored to an office desk can lose their luster.

### Oldsters, Pastors, Surrogates, and Missionaries

Older folks, while they are still active and have their health, are in a position to do wonderful mission work all over the world, as well as within the parish itself. They are in a position to be anchors to the young, especially those who live far from blood relatives. Our daughters both grew up an ocean away from kin, and there was a succession of older parishioners during their growing years who appointed themselves surrogate grandparents to our girls—this was a real blessing to us, to our girls, and to those elders who made that commitment. At a time when personal relationships are in such turmoil, these are indescribable gifts to many.

Then there are the elderly who are just natural pioneers. During the last few years, I have visited a number of new church plants. Almost invariably there have been at each newly planted congregation parishioners who are sixty and seventy years old, and for whom these new ventures are the focus of their Christian service. Even if the congregation to which they belong is not a brand-new one, older Christians of-

ten have the time and energy to pioneer all sorts of new and exciting
projects, in addition to the capacity of some to make significant financial contributions to the development of the work.

In the late eighties, while visiting East Africa, I was having dinner
with an English missionary who was then in her sixties. She was a little
starchy, but had a heart of pure gold, and was soon to complete her final tour of duty. She talked frankly about the adjustments that would
accompany her return to Britain for retirement. Over a meal in a colorful local restaurant, eating meats I had never tasted before, she shared
her vision to develop a ministry in the corner of England in which she
would be living that would touch the lives of seniors, the people the
British call old-age pensioners. She had been giving considerable
thought to this venture. It had an evangelistic, a spiritual, and a so-
cial/physical dimension. I lost touch with her after her retirement from
overseas service, and have always wondered what became of this dream.
Yet as I think back fondly to that fascinating African night, this is the
sort of vision we need to be nurturing.

However, it is vital that we create congregational communities that
welcome the elderly and are willing to become caregivers when these
senior citizens of the Kingdom decline physically to such an extent that
they can no longer either offer that helping hand or share in that ministry that has been their heart's desire for so long. One worrying aspect
of lively and active congregations is that they sometimes fall into the
temptation of not providing the type of pastoral care appropriate to
the elderly.

Yet even when Christians are no longer able to do many of the
things they used to do, they are often a tremendous source of prayer
and intercession in a parish. This, again, is something that congregations tend to overlook. Intercessory prayer has, somehow, been pushed
into the background in the mainline churches. Amidst all the talk of
centering prayer, spirituality, journaling, and so forth, that God longs
for an intercessory relationship with his people is easy to forget. Thankfully there is usually a small cadre of aging "prayer warriors" in the congregation who are willing to focus on this part of God's work.

Even if these older folks have not had much experience of intercessory prayer, unfettered by some of the burdens that keep the rest of us
running at high speed and with time on their hands, it is something
that many are able to pick up with relative ease—and it is far more satisfying than the inane diet of much daytime television. Some larger
congregations of various denominational traditions have not just
prayer chains, but also ministers of intercession who train and deploy

those who have that gift from God. Almost inevitably, it is senior Christians who are the stalwarts in this ministry.

## The Sandwich Generation

A complicating factor that parishes and ministries are going to have to address is the effect increased numbers of elderly, and greater longevity, will have on the traditional "sandwich generation." The "sandwich generation" is those trapped in the middle—men and women who juggle to attend to the needs of both old and young at the same time. Many a harassed parent finds life is often made more problematic by the distress caused by their own parents as they age, whether they live around the corner or on the other side of the globe.

During the first part of this new century, lengthened life expectancy means that for the first time in history there are as many as five generations in one congregation or family. Not only does this mean a wider array of ages to care for, but lives will be increasingly unsettled by the fact that mobility will have children, elderly, and then the caregiver generation living all over the map.

Until my mother died on Easter Day 2000, I was part of that generation. It does not take much imagination to work out how incredibly complex and stressful life can be when, like us, you live an ocean or a continent away from aging parents and the rest of the family. In the future, as life expectancy continues to lengthen as a result of the miracles of science and biotechnology, and as diverse family arrangements work themselves out, those in the middle will find themselves stretched to the limits and requiring pastoral care.

One further complication arises from the fact that historically the in-between generation has been the pool that has provided much of the active leadership in our parishes. With demands from all sides, it is going to be increasingly difficult for the sandwich generation to continue to provide both the leadership in church life that they have in the past, and to care for the needs of their extended family, or the hangers-on that will inevitably link themselves to stable family units. Although this is not a new issue, changing demographics mean that it needs to be addressed creatively by parishes.

## Christians Don't Retire

There is no simple solution to these challenges. However, I would like to propose a model that others could consider adapting for themselves. I am set to reach the age of sixty-five in the year 2010. Despite the fact that I could retire at that time, if not earlier, as a disciple of Jesus Christ who made solemn vows of Christian service at ordination, it does not seem appropriate to retire unless I am physically or psychologically no longer able to actively pursue God's calling.

Instead, I intend not only to keep my mind and body in good shape, but to provide support for the new generation of leaders in whatever way I can, and to minister as an active priest among my contemporaries. Today I meet a lot of ordained men and women who slide into the background when they let go of the formal ministry in which they have been engaged for much of their lives. I would hope that we could create an environment in which the skills and wisdom of both ordained and layleaders from the past can be used efficiently and effectively.

I trust that Social Security, savings, and income from our church's pension fund will be enough to help me meet my material needs—even if the payout from all of them is less proportionately than might have been the case with the present generation of elderly. In fact, present fiscal responsibility is partly driven by the fact that I want to be able to serve Christ actively well into my so-called golden years, and careful management of dollars now will allow for that. Given this facet of the demographic challenge, I hope that other Christians will see the possibilities and begin to act accordingly.

The age wave that is now bearing down upon us is an opportunity to serve Christ in our fellow men and women as they get older. It provides a setting within which older Christians can be given a new life and oriented to new forms of Christian service. As we look at these realities, our only limits will be the scope of our creativity and imaginations.

✦ ✦ ✦

### To Think and Talk Over

1. As your congregation ages, is it going to wither away or are the elderly set to be dynamic leaders?
2. What particular skills and insights do elderly people bring to ministry?
3. Is there anything in the area of ministry that an older person cannot do?
4. Talk about how the diverse lifestyles of the people who are now middle-aged are going to be carried over into their old age.
5. What sort of things do you think a Christian elder corps can do?
6. What do you think the role of older, retired priests ought to be?

7. What are the challenges facing the "sandwich generation," and how might a congregation help them to cope with those challenges?
8. Think about what a community of praying elders might look like.

### Suggestions for Further Reading

Dyctwald, Kenneth. *Age Wave: How the Most Important Trend of Our Time Will Change Our Future* (New York: Bantam Doubleday Dell, 1990).

Freedman, Marc. *Prime Time: How Baby Boomers Will Revolutionize Retirement and Transform America* (New York: Public Affairs, 2000).

Kaplan, Robert D. *An Empire Wilderness—Travels into America's Future* (New York: Random House, 1998).

Kennedy, Paul. *Preparing for the Twenty-first Century* (New York: Random House, 1993).

Knoke, William. *Bold New World—The Essential Roadmap to the Twenty-first Century* (New York: Kodansha America, 1996).

### Web Sites

- There are a lot of excellent links on ministry among the aging to be found at www.esmanet.com, the Web site of the Episcopal Society for Ministry on Aging.
- The National Senior Service Corps (NSSC) has a thirty-year history of leadership in senior volunteer service, and works with nearly half a million Americans who are over fifty-five in all fifty states. The NSSC is behind projects like the Foster Grandparents Program. They can be reached at the Corporation for National Service, whose Web site is www.cns.gov.
- Habitat for Humanity has done a tremendous job providing life-affirming activity for elders. Providing homes for the poor all over the nation and the world, this is one of those big challenges that can really catch the imagination. Their Web site is www.habitat.org.
- Marc Freedman's book *Prime Time* has a multi-page appendix of organizations, movements, and agencies working to provide a new approach to retirement, complete with Web sites, addresses, and telephone numbers. This is one of the most valuable resources for focusing on ministry among elders that I have come across.

# TREND SEVEN
# An Array of Impossible Moral Dilemmas

> *We are entering a super renaissance—a time when we are changing life, creating life, linking people together much closer and faster, changing the meaning of reality, time, space, and location. We are about to design and manipulate matter, and are on the edge of tapping the greatest energy resource in the universe. What will this all mean to us as human beings?*[1]
>
> John L. Petersen, futurist

## Beyond Culture Wars

Among other things, the last two decades of the twentieth century turned out to be a veritable battlefield of issues, both within the church and in the wider culture. James Davidson Hunter of the University of Virginia identified and tracked many of the components of this reality as it emerged, and wrote a startling book that drew our attention to what was happening as ideological polarization set in, making the social and moral issues of our time the theater of war. The resulting ideological struggles have turned into round after round of what Hunter called "culture wars."[2]

Not surprisingly, we enter the twenty-first century with almost none of these issues resolved, especially those related to the issues of human sexuality and reproduction. There does seem to be a slight diminution of the influence of single-issue organizations that have been the primary foot soldiers of these ongoing culture wars, and some of the bitter fizz seems to have gone out of conflicts over issues like abortion. But tensions are always lurking; they are seldom far beneath the surface. This could be but a temporary lull, because larger and more ominous clouds loom on the horizon and are bearing down on us as fast as a tornado.

If you thought the moral dilemmas that confronted us in the 1990s were hard to handle, fasten your seat belts, because, as they say, you ain't seen nothing yet. The massive issues that are barreling down the pike in our direction have the potential to be even more divisive and will force us to think harder and longer about our presuppositions—something we seldom do at the moment.

It is my hope that the size, number, and scope of the issues will drive us to our knees, to an ardent and honest study of the Scriptures, to the tradition in which we are rooted, and to our intelligence, to learning, and common sense. I am certain that future moral dilemmas will produce some strange bedfellows. For instance, individuals who, say, might have found themselves on opposite sides of the abortion battles or may have disagreed about how to approach issues of race, could now suddenly discover themselves in agreement over the worrisome possibilities that accompany the cloning of human beings.

The Catholic lay scholar Peter Kreeft has drawn attention to the way that alliances can change radically in his startlingly titled *Ecumenical Jihad*. In the book's introduction he asks us to listen to his contention that circumstances and ideologies are changing so fast that old categories often no longer make much sense when confronted with new realities. "One of (my) main points . . . is that we need to change our current categories and our current alignments." We need to realize, first, that we are at war and, second, that the sides have changed radically: "Many of our former enemies (for example, Muslims) are now our friends, and some of our former friends (for example, humanists) are now our enemies." He goes on to state that alliances are tactical, not theoretical. "Allies do not give up their sovereignty or their individuality. They simply put their disputes on hold for tactical, practical reasons. Such tactical moves are matters of prudential wisdom."[3]

Whether we like it or not, scientific discovery is advancing at such a pace that it is remaking the world. The communications revolution has been the launch pad for certain facets of this brave new culture, but other scientific innovations have been bubbling for a long time and are now reaching a point where theory is becoming reality. Nanotechnology, for example—the creation of mechanisms that enable us to construct or reconstruct entities a molecule at a time—is on the verge of emerging as a major force. Eric Drexler, the man who coined the term "nanotech," is so certain that this will have profound implications that he has said that "twentieth-century technology is headed for the junk heap."[4]

This century could well see great advances in fusion research and the creation of almost limitless power resources, while extraordinary advances in cybernetics and robotics could mean that within a couple of generations the machines will have the upper hand, because they will be more intelligent. Software and microprocessor designer Bill Joy, who has been one of the primary developers of the Java software language, has now cast himself in the role of cyber guru, is asking substantial questions about the work in which he has been involved. He realized that we are moving along a path where highly intelligent machines would be making decisions for themselves, which ultimately would mean that the fate of the human race would be at the mercy of these machines.

> With the prospect of human-level computing power in about thirty years, a new idea suggests itself: that I may be working to create tools which will enable the construction of the technology that may replace our species. How do I feel about this? Very uncomfortable . . . Given the incredible power of these new technologies, shouldn't we be asking how we can coexist with them? . . . We may not survive the encounter with the superior robot species. How soon could such an intelligent robot be built? The coming advances in computing power seem to make it possible by 2030. And once an intelligent robot exists, it is only a small step to a robot species—to an intelligent robot that can make evolved copies of itself.[5]

Then there is always the possibility of machine and human merging in certain ways—as a result, the Borg on Star Trek may not be all that far-fetched. Furthermore, it is entirely likely that exploration could very well begin taking humankind on a journey that could eventually lead our race out of the confines of this solar system. All of these and other "advances" will provide the human race and Christian believers with enormous ethical and moral conundrums, yet immediate pressure on our principles could come from the burgeoning field of biogenetics.

Because of the extraordinary advances being made in understanding the nature of life, biotechnology is the discipline most likely to raise the trickiest questions with which Christians will be forced to wrestle in the coming few decades. The majority of issues that are going to cause the most distress will be the ones focused on the very meaning and nature of life itself. The dilemmas surrounding issues such as abortion and euthanasia are in the process of becoming a lot more complex. Whole new dimensions are rearing their heads as science continues its helter-skelter advances on so many fronts.

### The Human Genome Project and Beyond

Progress on the mapping of the human genome by both publicly and privately funded scientists and researchers involved in the Human Genome Project is moving so rapidly that during the course of the writing of this book the first "rough draft" of human DNA has become available—far sooner than anyone had expected.[6] These extraordinary findings are merely the first step in our ability to literally re-engineer human beings. While these discoveries are in some respects full of promise, suggesting that it is within our grasp to relieve some of the worst medical problems that have dogged our race for centuries, they have an incredibly dark side that is going to challenge humanity to the utmost through most of this century.

While researchers are the first to admit that there is a tremendous amount about the human genome that we do not know, this is the first step on a journey that has incredible implications. In due course we will understand the biochemical code for human genes, however many there turn out to be, and locating them within the twenty-three chromosomes in the human genome may turn out to be the necessary first step to solving most of these mysteries.

> The hope is that the completed genome will enable scientists to lay bare the genetic triggers for hundreds of diseases—from Alzheimer's to diabetes to heart disease—and to devise exquisitely sensitive diagnostic tests. It will help pharmaceutical companies create drugs tailored to a patient's genetic profile, boosting effectiveness while drastically reducing side effects. It could change our very conception of what a disease is, replacing broad descriptive categories—breast cancer, for example—with precise genetic definitions that make diagnosis sure and treatment swift.[7]

While everything in this *Time* magazine report sounds fine and dandy, it is not difficult to see the dark side of such discoveries. You are not particularly enthusiastic about abortion? Neither am I. But have you ever thought of the moral dilemmas that confront us when we talk about our potential capacity to enable a couple to sit down with their doctor and "boutique" design the baby of their choice? We are not talking just in terms of making sure that a baby is not born with Down's syndrome, nor of the gender we prefer, we are thinking about the molding and shaping of this potential human's personality, tastes, intelligence, and so forth. While it is likely that we will soon be able to undertake massive manipulations of genes while babies are still in utero (or before), we do not know or understand the long-term effects of such, dare I use the word, "eugenics."

There might be great promise in the potential to eliminate certain genetic problems—like sickle cell anemia or other hereditary abnormalities, but how long will it be before we find ourselves being put under subtle pressure to fashion unborn children so they have the characteristics that we (or an overbearing larger community) want them to have? And who decides? We could also find ourselves reaching a point where genetic scans of unborn children will lead to increasing penalties against those parents who are not prepared to terminate the development of "imperfect" children—like the removal of health insurance coverage, or the addition of intolerable riders. Meanwhile, the lives of socially unacceptable children could be made impossible as a domineering culture driven by economics alone shapes values, rather than honoring the dignity of every human life, no matter its health or shape when it enters the world.

*Newsweek,* in its coverage of the Human Genome Project in the spring of 2000, reported the following:

> The easier it is to change ourselves and our children, the less society may tolerate those who do not, warns Lori Andrews of Kent College of Law. If genetic tests in utero predict mental dullness, obesity, short stature—or other undesirable traits of the moment—will society disparage children whose parents let them be born with those traits? Already Andrews finds, some nurses and doctors blame parents for bringing into the world a child whose birth defect was diagnosable before delivery; how long will it be before the same condemnation applies to cosmetic imperfections?[8]

In an interview with Rodney Clapp in the summer of 1998 published in *Books and Culture,* Stanley Hauerwas of Duke University suggested that in one hundred years from what might distinguish

Christians from the run-of-the-mill culture is that they could be the only subgroup within society who have an appropriate grasp of the sanctity of all human life.[9] While Hauerwas is famous for his outspokenness and overstatement, his comments challenge us to focus on some of the long-term implications of developments that are currently in their infancy. We will have to struggle mightily with huge bioethical issues before the twenty-first century is very old—so to be forewarned is to be forearmed.

While I am always a little dubious of Christians with paranoid tendencies—those who claim we are on the verge of overt persecution in the West—this is an area where Christians (and most other theists) are likely to find themselves increasingly up against the mood of the prevailing culture. Christians may hope that the prevailing culture will conclude that the theistic understanding of the sanctity of life, however malformed, predominates, but given the drift of the culture in the last fifty years we can in no way guarantee this.

The kind of pressures that will be brought upon people to conform could be financial. Already there is a growing body of evidence that as the potentials of costly disease are being uncovered by genetic testing, insurance companies are making life difficult for patients. While a majority of states have passed laws prohibiting discrimination on the basis of genetic testing, many of the laws enacted have loopholes, providing fragile protection to every one of us as more information becomes readily accessible about our individual genomes.

Should there be a clash between a society that has entirely disconnected itself from its Judeo-Christian roots and its Christian, Jewish, and Muslim citizens, then believers need to be prepared to find themselves and their attitudes increasingly less tolerated. This is where stories like C. S. Lewis's *That Hideous Strength* have an awful lot to teach us—in that book Lewis makes it clear that there can be a deep malevolence in scientific discovery when it is misconceived and misused.

### How about Cloning Then?

If the moral consequences associated with the manipulation of genes as a result of the discoveries that are beginning to cascade out of the Human Genome Project and the rise of gene therapies are going to be enormous, the advent of cloning raises another huge set of problems. Although most researchers have for the moment publicly distanced themselves from the acceptability of cloning human life, forecasters suggest that, whether we like it or not, this will happen during this decade—some even suggest within the first year or two of the new millennium. Science fiction writer and keen observer Arthur C. Clarke predicts that the first publicly admitted human cloning is likely to take place by 2004 at the latest.[10]

Once again, all sorts of ontological questions about the nature of life and its sanctity are brought to the fore by this possibility. Meanwhile, it is clear that researchers do not understand the long-term consequences both physically and to the personality of the cloned individual—there has been some anxiety among those who cloned Dolly the sheep that her cell structures are prematurely aging. The consequences of applying untried medical procedures to humans can be seen in the lives of thousands of middle-aged men and women on both sides of the Atlantic Ocean whose bodies are badly disfigured due to each of their mother's use of the drug thalidomide while pregnant. Their struggles should be a huge warning to us as we take steps into another medical unknown.

Theologians Scott B. Rae and Paul M. Cox explore the profound ethical consequences of cloning in their book *Bioethics—A Christian Approach in a Pluralistic Age.* Observing that science fiction writers have got considerable mileage out of the potential of cloning, they remark that the process for the "cloning of embryos in the lab does not appear to present any problems per se, since researchers are merely reproducing in the lab the natural process that occurs in the body when identical twins or triplets are produced."

However, the process becomes more problematic when embryos created for scientific purposes "are either fatally damaged during the research process or discarded after the research is finished." Furthermore, they question the appropriateness of creating cloned embryos for "health insurance" or the cloning of embryos for purchase and sale on the open market. "It does not take much imagination to see the appeal of the genetic material of well-endowed athletes or models and the attraction of such a product on the open market."[11]

Every time I read of some new advance in such sensitive arenas as these, I find my mind pondering the message behind the story of the Tower of Babel (Genesis 11:1–9). Could it be that our race has gone too far, and is now arrogantly reaching into realms that belong to God alone—a God whose values are hardly admitted by those on this relentless pursuit of discovery? It would appear that research is advancing at such a pace that our ethical understanding of its consequences is unable to keep up with the moral outcome of our actions. Meanwhile, there seems to be a limited number within the churches who are bringing these concerns to the fore—whatever their theological bias.

A further issue with which we are going to have to deal is that of cybernetic implants. We are reaching a point where mechanical "additives" are moving beyond new and improved heart pacemakers to discovering how to grow fresh limbs, even store human memory and personality in a database until such time as new bodies can be generated to "house" this identity. To some this may sound ludicrous, like a bad sci-fi nightmare, but there is already research going on that could lead in this direction.

### To Understand and to Find Moral Ways Forward

While avoiding thoughtless knee-jerk reactions that prefer ignorance to discovery, it is important that we learn what is going on, and then seek to understand its advisability in the light of God's revelation. Given that huge numbers of Christians do not allow themselves even to think about such demanding issues, it is likely that many of the well-worn arguments that have surrounded the abortion debate will take on new significance and shape in the years ahead. What worries me is that so shrill will be the shouts of anti-intellectualism coming from a large segment of American Christianity and so politicized will these issues become that even legitimate scientific advances could be rejected out of hand.

We should encourage congregations and judicatories of the historic denominations to take seriously the need to educate themselves about what is happening, and then study appropriate ways in which we as Christians might respond to these changing circumstances. It is also to be hoped that we would have the intelligence to grasp some of the nuances that will necessarily accompany our reactions.

There are so many ethical issues and dilemmas that our culture is incubating that we have the space to focus on only a handful here. I have chosen to glance at the issues in the world of medicine and the sanctity of human life to illustrate the extraordinary intellectual and moral challenges that are already bearing down upon us. Every day there is such an enormous flow of new discoveries that it would take an army of analysts to keep us fully informed of what is going on. However, it is vital that we do not bury our heads in the sand and ignore what is happening until it is too late. It is imperative that Christians attempt to understand at least some of what is going on, to undertake appropriate theological reflection in light of these facts, and then to grapple with all that these things mean if we are to continue honoring the image of God in humankind, and the sacredness of human life.

I could have spent as much time asking us to consider cybernetics, or whether technology itself is morally neutral. Most of us tend to get "gee whiz" enamored when it comes to the way technology advances. It is fun to see what brand-new advances in the computer sciences can do, but is there a shadowy underside that we are ignoring? I have a sense that there is, and that it should be something we spend more time talking about. If it is new, clever, or exciting, then we will attach ourselves to whatever it is without realizing that it may have the power to subvert both our faith and our values. Individual privacy is also something that will become increasingly compromised.

Without realizing it, by being uncritical, are we giving in to the "principalities and powers" who have the capacity to nuzzle their way into our hearts like warm puppies, which then grow up to be bloodthirsty and destructive pit bulls? The late Bishop Lesslie Newbigin did a lot of thinking about the agenda that the principalities and powers have inserted into our culture.

> The principalities and powers are realities. We may not be able to visualize them, to locate them, or to say exactly what they are. But we are foolish if we pretend that they do not exist. Certainly one cannot read the Gospels without recognizing that the ministry of Jesus from beginning to end was a mighty spiritual battle with powers which are not simply human frailties, errors, diseases, or sins . . . If we try to systematize the diffuse and flexible language of the (New Testament) writers and develop a sort of systematic demonology, we shall . . . go astray. But if we live in the real world and take the Bible as our clue for understanding and coping with it, we shall certainly know what it means that our wrestling is not against flesh and blood but against invisible principalities and powers, and we shall learn what it means to put on the whole armor of God for the conflict.[12]

It would be wise for large parishes, ecumenical consortia of congregations, dioceses, and judicatories to set up panels of Christians to begin exploring the implications of some of the various scientific developments that are reshaping our world, while also putting them within their spiritual context. Among our parishioners we have many learned people whose insights will help us to understand and respond reasonably to this facet of the changing face of our world. Too often in the past, the church has been "caught with its pants down" and has responded reactively rather than proactively to new developments. The new knowledge that is coming to the forefront in our time is too important, and has too many long-term implications, for us to put all this on the back burner.

### Science and the Presence of God

As we have seen, there are many more areas of human endeavor that are raising a whole ocean of questions over which we Christians will be forced to puzzle. Some of them are exciting and encouraging, like the steady flow of new data coming from biochemistry, astrophysics, mathematics, and other disciplines that seem to be affirming the anthropic principle—that is, that there is an omnipotent designing mind behind the universe, and that the universe has been created that it be welcoming to intelligent life like our own.

Other areas raise huge unanswered or unanswerable questions—like the impact our species is having on the world's climate; whether we have any right as stewards of God's generosity to accelerate the extinction of any species; or the advisability and feasibility of seeking to contact any other intelligent life that might exist elsewhere in our galaxy. Some of these questions may seem far-fetched and fantastical, but they demand that we work hard to find a reasonable and ethically appropriate way forward.

I suspect that in the face of such a welter of new information and discovery, there will be believers who start walking away from any and all advances, becoming latter-day Amish who abandon computers rather than buttons, or Luddites who are determined to destroy every advance that comes down the tracks. Then there are those who are so enamored that they will swallow whatever they are presented assuming that such progress is at the worst neutral and at the best good. It is vital that thoughtful Christians be prepared to learn, debate, and explore, discovering where lines might need to be drawn, and then to lead the rest of us in joining the wider debate or making sometimes unpopular stands that are honoring to Christ and his Gospel.

Thoughtful scientists and technologists are admitting in greater numbers that it is not always easy to see the impact of what you are doing when you are in the midst of the vortex of change, and what one calls "the rapture of discovery." Bill Joy, the scientist and cyber guru quoted earlier in the chapter, goes on to say, "We have long been driven by the overarching desire to know that is the nature of science's quest, not stopping to notice that the progress to newer and more powerful technologies can take on a life of its own."[13]

It would seem, then, that if those making life-altering discoveries are unlikely to reflect on the implications of what they are doing, it is up to the Christian community to step in and become society's conscience in some way or another. Yet it is worrying right now to see what little thought most Christians and congregations have even given to all this. This is clearly an enormous challenge upon which we need to get up to speed.

I find myself wondering whether part of our tentativeness when it comes to such challenges is that we do not want to become embroiled in another battle as heavily politicized as the whole pro-life/pro-choice debate has become. If this is the case, it means that very often we are not able to see the real issues for the contemporary political trees that stand in the way. While this may be human nature coupled with the American way of doing things, some of the issues that will confront us in the future will require us to lay aside some of our more socially conditioned presuppositions.

✦ ✦ ✦

### To Think and Talk Over

1.  Make a list of the moral and ethical issues that you think might challenge us during the twenty-first century. Which ones do you think will be the most troubling, and why?
2.  Is there a point where it is necessary for Christians to walk away from scientific advances?
3.  Discuss Stanley Hauerwas's comment, "Within a hundred years, Christians may be known as those odd people who don't kill their children or their elderly."
4.  Look at Genesis 11:1–9. Do you think there are any parallels between the story of the Tower of Babel and the circumstances in which we find ourselves today? If so, why?
5.  Look at Ephesians 6:12ff, and look at the world in which we live. What do you think are the "principalities and powers" of our time?
6.  How do you think a congregation can keep up with the challenges

being presented by moral and ethical issues associated with scientific advance?

### Suggestions for Further Reading

Drexler, K. Eric. *Engines of Creation—The Coming Era of Nanotechnology* (New York: Doubleday/Anchor Press, 1986).
Negroponte, Nicholas. *Being Digital* (New York: Alfred A. Knopf, 1995).
Newbigin, Lesslie. *The Gospel in a Pluralist Society* (London and Grand Rapids, MI: SPCK and Wm. B. Eerdmans Publishing Co., 1989).
Petersen, John L. *The Road to 2015* (Corte Madera: Waite Group Press, 1994).
Rae, Scott B., and Cox, Paul M. *Bioethics: A Christian Approach in a Pluralistic Age* (Grand Rapids, MI: Wm. B. Eerdmans Publishing Co., 1999).
Sine, Tom. *Mustard Seed Versus McWorld* (Grand Rapids, MI: Baker Book House, 1999).
Wink, Walter. *The Powers That Be* (New York: Galilee Doubleday, 1998).
*Wired* magazine is also an excellent resource. (See http://www.wired.com.)

### Web Sites

- An excellent Web site for the study of medically related ethical topics is that of the Christian Medical Fellowship in Britain. Not only are there excellent studies on such topics as human cloning there, but there is a posting of papers that have been presented to the British government by the Christian Medical Fellowship, or the government's boards of enquiry, committees, etc. It can be found at www.cmf.org.uk.
- If you want to get up-to-the-minute information about the Human Genome Project, you will find www-ls.lanl.gov/HGhotlist.html an excellent place to begin. It is a list of the Human Genome Most Used Links. The official site of the National Human Genome Research Institute is www.nhgri.nih.gov.
- Rae and Cox's book *Bioethics: A Christian Approach in a Pluralistic Age* is part of a series produced under the auspices of the Center for Bioethics and Human Dignity. Information about the Center can be found at their Web site, www.bioethix.org.
- If you want to discover what some of the ethical issues before us in

our culture are today, there is an enormous amount of information that can be found at a secular site: www.omega23.com. This links directly to Amazon.com, and will enable you to purchase any number of books on the various topics.

- To learn more about nanotechnology, you will find an enormous amount of information at http://nanotech.rutgers.edu/nanotech/papers/update1.htmlNanotechnologyMIT.

# TREND EIGHT
# The Continuing Spirituality Boom

*Ten years ago, people were inclined to dismiss the Church as dull, boring, old-fashioned, or irrelevant, today an increasing chorus is insisting the Church is "unspiritual." It is not always easy to define what 'spirituality' might mean in this context . . . but it is obvious that if the Church is the last place today's spiritual searchers will go for spirituality, then Christians face a major problem of credibility and integrity.*[1]
John Drane, theology professor and pastor

### Spirituality Crept Up While We Weren't Looking

*The Futurist* is published six times a year by the World Future Society, and is dedicated to the study of what tomorrow could to look like. I have been an avid reader of this journal for more years than I care to remember, but I have been surprised by how long it took the editors, whom one would expect to be people of perspicacity and great foresight, to catch up with the changing spiritual realities in the culture. It seemed evident that their distinctly secular perspective had blinded them to what was going on beneath the spiritual surface—and then bubbling over volcanically.

Even when they did start coming to terms with it, their coverage was limpid and apologetic, with almost all their focus on New Age and kindred movements, and little interest in the Judeo-Christian tradition. By their silence they were, in effect, saying that little was going on in the churches that has any relevance—perhaps like so many others steeped in Enlightenment thinking, they were just waiting for the traditional religion to shrivel. Even today, when on odd occasions the churches are raised in this serious and usually pretty objective publication, the attitude toward them is off hand or dismissive. Churches are leftovers from yesterday—irrelevant, meaningless, dying, or so it seems. A huge number of otherwise thoughtful futurists are so caught up in discovery and the impact new technology might have that they either cannot or will not see the vast spiritual burgeoning that has been taking place.

One of the great paradoxes of the last twenty to thirty years is how the strongly secularizing trends that accompany globalization, rather than destroying spirituality as many had expected, have stirred up spiritual fervor almost everywhere in the world. The Charismatic Renewal, the resurgence of Eastern Orthodoxy and Evangelicalism, Islamic Fundamentalism, and the rise of the diversity of fellow travelers in the New Age movement are all different facets of this process. Hindus in India are rediscovering their spiritual roots, as are young Jews in Israel and from profoundly secular homes in America.

I love the way Tom Wright, Canon Theologian at Westminster Abbey, London, puts it. "Following the long winter of secularism, in which most people gave up believing in anything religious or spiritual, the current revival of spiritualities of all sorts is an inevitable swing of the pendulum, a cultural shift in which people have been able once more to celebrate a dimension of human existence that the Enlightenment had marginalized. But one cannot assume that what people mean by *god* or *spirit, religion,* or *spirituality* within these movements bears very much relation to Christianity."[2]

In their recent book, *The Next American Spirituality*, George Gallup and Timothy Jones tell us that their intensive polling results and observations overwhelmingly confirm that "never in recent memory has spirituality seemed to be so much on people's minds. And the ferment and activity show no signs of abating. We expect more of the same. Amid healthy expressions and bogus claims, whether life-changing or flaky, whatever its warm promise and its sometime quirkiness, spirituality is here to stay."[3]

They are right and are by no means alone in their observations. Faith Popcorn, one of the trendiest of America's futures analysts and very much a "material girl," writes that more and more people are "looking for the meaning of Life, seeking the answers to the Big Questions. Why now, and not at any other point in our recent history? you may wonder. Because collectively, we're digging deep into our memory, searching for some leap of faith, some link of primal instinct, to help us cut through the daily chaos . . ."[4]

### Even Science Is Changing Its Tune

In a relatively short time, the whole spiritual landscape in the West has been changed beyond recognition. We now belong to a culture that is no longer confident in the answers being offered by a rationalistic and earth-bound understanding of science. After several hundred years in abeyance, not only are we willing to look beyond ourselves, but we are realizing that science itself, far from disproving the existence of God, seems to be pointing toward a designing hand that has created and is sustaining the universe.

Patrick Glynn was a confirmed atheist for many years. He studied philosophy at a number of the world's great universities and holds a Ph.D. in philosophy from Harvard. Some years ago he reached the point where external and internal pressures drove him to re-examine the emerging evidence. Writing in the mid-nineties, he said,

> Over the past twenty years, a significant body of evidence has emerged, shattering the foundations of the long-dominant modern secular worldview. These new discoveries, it seems to me, add up to a powerful—indeed, all-but-incontestable—case for what once was considered a completely debatable matter of "faith": the existence of soul, afterlife, and God. I came upon these new discoveries rather late in the game—long after I had decided, on the basis of intensive philosophical study, that there was no God in a personal sense, no afterlife, no souls.[5]

Glynn penned these words just as what has become known as the "intelligent design" movement was beginning to gather force, and increasing amounts of research, in fields as diverse as microbiology to astrophysics, were pointing ever more clearly in the direction of a creating deity of some kind. Certainly, these new insights into creation are having a noticeable impact on the level of confidence that many people place in the veracity of materialistic and secular worldviews. These had seemed to carry all before them for several hundred years, but now in many quarters have been bloodied and are in full retreat.

During the time that this book was being written, Canada's leading science fiction writer, Robert J. Sawyer, published his novel *Calculating God*. A thoughtful and well read writer whose tales reflect a rich grounding in technology, contemporary discovery, and philosophical reflection, Sawyer uses the arrival of an alien scientist, a Forhilnor from a planet in the Beta Hydri system, at the Royal Ontario Museum in

Toronto, to explore in terms accessible to the average reader the whole notion of "intelligent design." The book is one of his most fascinating, yet, a good yarn with a great deal to chew on. It is in this kind of way that ideas become common currency.

It is difficult to say how long these levels of spiritual sensitivity that are emerging alongside this new intellectual awareness will last. I suspect the intensity of this spiritual ferment will go on for at least another fifteen to twenty years, and then gradually will merge into some kind of new synthesis that accepts a spiritual dimension of some kind as normative. Much depends on how all the components of this play against one another, and the effect that they have upon the wider culture.

What has made this spiritual ferment more complex for North Americans (and most other Westerners) is the diversity of spiritualities that are now "available" to them. When spiritual awakenings took place in the past, because the then Christian world was insulated from other faith traditions, the choices available to Western spiritual searchers were competing brands of Christianity, but now a whole smorgasbord of religious and spiritual options has started to emerge. The Christian faith is now just one of a number of viable belief systems—and must compete with everyone else for its "market share."

Among other things, adherents of a diversity of religious traditions have migrated into North America. We in Canada and the United States have yet to come to terms with the potential consequences of this infusion of religious ideas. Iowa boasts a significant Islamic population; in the sprawling southern suburbs of Vancouver, British Columbia, there are huge megatemples of various Eastern faiths; while the heavily Baptist county where I have been living in Tennessee has a growing population of Buddhists, Muslims, Wiccans, and Hindus! These faiths, and certain homegrown varieties of believing, make them an object of curious fascination to tens of thousands.[6]

Our highly individualistic, atomized, and fragmented culture is desperate for some footing beyond itself. The popular spiritualities that have emerged tend to be highly subjective and have a strong individualistic "feel-good factor," reflecting a mix-and-match approach to the world of both soul and body. Nevertheless, somewhere beneath all these "warm fuzzies" there is a yearning for something deeper, something more.

George Gallup and Tim Jones talk about this as "America's Epic Soul Quest." Whether your spiritual goal is salvation, nirvana, enlightenment, good karma, or merely inner peace, there are many more choices of churches and tenets than ever before. Yet, despite the fact that some are on a journey that involves the eternal dimension, a large component of the spirituality boom is more about creating a warm "buzz" than pursuing those sometimes demanding disciplines that are rooted in human religious history. Gallup and Jones think that our culture fosters spiritualities that exalt the self and downplay God, that elevate our needs and whims and neglect divine mystery and sovereignty.

> What is happening around us is opening people to genuine searching. One of the authors once asked Martin Marty, professor of modern Christianity at the University of Chicago, if he felt the modern soul fascination was authentic. "The hunger is always authentic," he answered. "It's just that you can feed it with Twinkies or with broccoli."[7]

In the last generation we saw fads like Scientology become a significant force—especially in movieland, while more significant faiths like Buddhism, varieties of Hinduism, Islam, and native American faiths have begun to prosper in North America—and not just on the North American continent. The editor of *Tricycle,* a somewhat trendy Buddhist publication, claims more than 150,000 readers, while Native American dream catchers, ceremonial pipes, and rain sticks are to be found everywhere.

This same ferment is going on in Europe. There are geographical dioceses of the Church of England where probably more worshippers attend Friday prayers in mosques than are to be found in parish churches on Sunday. France, also, is a prime target for Islamic evangelization, while Wicca and all sorts of other romanticized and imagined re-creations of pre-Christian faiths are on the rise everywhere. "Today, it is no problem to find practicing shamans in the main streets of Western cities, while statistics show that in the former West Germany alone there are something like 90,000 registered witches and wizards."[8]

### Give Me That On-line Religion

If all this sounds confusing, then log on and surf some of the spirituality sites present in cyberspace. Keep your eyes open for further diversification and the marketing of spiritualities of all kinds on the Internet —reaching far beyond the developed world, where its presence has now become a part of everyday life. If you want to discover what is happening online, then go to your Web browser and type in topics such as "god," "goddess," "pagan," "spirituality," and so forth, punch the enter button and see what turns up. Within a few seconds you will be shown thousands of Web sites that are hawking the most bewildering range of bizarre spiritual ideas.

One of the most predictable faith factors during the next couple of decades will be a multiplication of cyberchurches and cyberreligions, many of which will be distinctly quirky. This will be the wild side of the Internet, which goes far beyond exploring the inner child that so entranced Boomers seeking to fill their inner void, channeling with aliens from outer space, or macabre and syncretistic variants on the historic paganism that lies in our Western past. These will surely start impacting Christian congregations in the West, especially those that have only a loose grasp on creedal orthodoxy. Since the Internet is global, these spiritual forces are likely to be mixed and matched with religious notions and ideas that have originated in the rich diversity of ethnic and regional faiths to be found all over the world.

Because so many of the "new faiths" that will be born from the Internet or out of today's intense human search are likely to be peculiar and unique, not many are likely to survive very long. However, there is no accounting for the gullibility of seemingly intelligent human beings when it comes to seeking answers to life's ultimate questions—or inner peace and meaning. I have to admit that a number of years ago when I first came across L. Ron Hubbard's then nascent religion, Scientology, I never expected it to be on the scene as such a powerful force for so long, yet it is thriving in certain quarters. Countless new scientologist-style religions are being dreamed up every month, some of which could well begin making an impact.

Yet, as far as Christians are concerned, all is not lost to this new wave of spiritual ferment. These movements certainly challenge the Christian faith, but "church leader after leader reports great and growing interest in more than a secondhand, long-distance relationship with God. Millions of American Christians are drawn to prayer meetings, spiritual growth weekends, and Bible study groups. Gatherings for prayer and extended periods of fasting have drawn record numbers. In the last year of the 1990s, three million school-age young people and their teachers gathered for "See You at the Pole" prayer rallies at their school flagpoles."[9] It would seem that Christianity is far from down-and-out in our culture.

Yet although Christianity still has much to learn if it is to function effectively in this utterly different spiritual climate, the faith has deep and abiding resources that speak movingly and meaningfully to the human soul. Eugene Peterson says, "'Ecstasy doesn't last,' wrote novelist E. M. Forster, 'but it cuts a channel for something lasting.' Single-minded, persevering faithfulness confirms the authenticity of our spirituality. The ancestors we look to for encouragement in this business—Augustine of Hippo and Julian of Norwich, John Calvin and Amy Carmichael, John Bunyan and Teresa of Avila—didn't flit. They *stayed*."[10] During the last two or three years there has been some evidence that there are spiritual searchers who have started to grow tired of the trendy, feel-good faiths they have been dabbling with and are beginning to look for something that is rooted and has staying power.

### New Religious Wars?

There is a significant and worrying flip side to this multihued spiritual explosion: religious conflict. As we look at all these emerging spiritual alternatives, even the least trained eye can see that they are not all going in the same direction, and furthermore often their tenets are at sharp odds with one another. Again, you do not need to be a rocket scientist to see the potential for conflict in such diversity, living as we do, cheek by jowl in densely populated cities and ever closer electronic proximity with billions of others around the world.

It is little wonder that Postmodernity has sought to prize tolerance above all else. We live today in a society of comparative relatives, a society that has come to consider intolerance of others, their beliefs, and their lifestyles, as the greatest of all sins. Given the unimaginable extent of our diversity, this is hardly surprising. Part of the rationale seems to be that if we can find out how to tolerate one another no matter what we think or believe, then this cacophony of convictions can continue to coexist side-by-side without our coming to blows.

This excessive drive toward tolerance is also the inevitable product of a culture that, as it has loosened its attachment to Judeo-Christian principles, is letting go of its grasp on the notion that there might be such things as absolutes and inalienable truths. These days truth has become relative to the community in which we participate. This "Postmodern worldview operates with a community-based understanding of truth. It affirms whatever we accept is true, and even the ways we envision truth are dependent on the community in which we participate. Further, and far more radically, the Postmodern worldview affirms that this relativity extends beyond our *perceptions* of truth to its essence: There is no absolute truth."[11]

"Religious encounters are inevitable in a pluralistic world," writes the Vatican's Archbishop Marcello Zago, but he concludes that the manner in which we have managed religious diversity in the past has become antiquated. "The American experiment to place religious allegiance in parentheses was possible in the past when American society was dominated by an overwhelmingly Christian culture, predominantly Protestant. With the coming of a very varied and widespread pluralism and given each person's instinct for promoting his or her own identity, both of which are reflected in religion, the previous methodology, although substantially positive, is no longer adequate."[12]

One possible way to head off potentially violent religious conflict is for all religious traditions to educate themselves about the nature of one another's faiths. As we mutually come to understand different religionists better, then at least we will be able to grasp the values that motivate their lives and their actions—and make allowances. Coming to terms with living in a diverse culture that is more overt in its affirmation of the spiritual and the unseen, one of the priorities of Christian education for both adults and children is to give Christians some notion of what the other religious traditions of the world stand for—both historical and newly minted faiths. This, of course, needs to be coupled with a much more significant formation of believers in our own faith, so that they are able to see the differences more clearly, make comparisons, and learn to live beside other faith traditions.

I fear, however, given the fallenness of humankind, that at some point something will trigger a reaction against the climate of overbearing tolerance in our time. I suspect we will see faith-inspired outbursts that will increasingly shock us—much as the wars of religion in Europe following the Reformation shocked thoughtful and sensitive men and women of those times, triggering a desire to create the kind of earthbound intellectual systems that came to full flower in the Enlightenment.

Christians in various parts of the world are already coming up against such opposition. In the Indian subcontinent, for example, simmering antagonisms toward Christians have been fanned into flame by militant Hindus in India and their Muslim counterparts in Pakistan. Meanwhile Christians in many Middle East and Central Asian Islamic areas have found it necessary to migrate away from their homelands in surprising numbers due to the intolerances they have experienced at the hands of the majority. Then there are the trials of the Balkans in the last ten to fifteen years that remind us the same tensions seethe beneath the surface in European life. A major question is whether violent religious intolerance will find its way to our shores in a big way, and if it does, what form it will take.

Furthermore, religious tension could have ominous overtones as we look at the global scene. Since World War II an exceptionally large proportion of the regional military hostilities have occurred around the fringes of the Islamic world. Not only is Islam feeling a surge of inner self-confidence, it also senses that it is being threatened by the rampant secularity that accompanies globalization. The tendency is, probably correctly, to point accusing fingers at the West for this state of affairs. There seems to be deep within the heart of Islamic faith a systemic animosity toward the modern world that has emerged. One wag has suggested one of Islam's problems is that it has yet to come to terms with the nineteenth century, let alone the twentieth or twenty-first—maybe there is a grain of truth in this comment.

Westerners cannot ignore Islam, or write it off as a phenomenon to be found primarily in the Arab world, or Central and East Asia. The Islamic faith has become global, and it is mushrooming in North America as a result of immigration, conversion of those disillusioned with their own historic tradition, and the relatively high birthrate in Muslim families vis-à-vis the mainline population. During this decade Islam looks set to surpass Judaism as the second largest religion of the U.S.A. We need to ask ourselves what this will mean for America's future, and for the future relationships between these two competing faiths.

Many Christians have, alas, already demonized the Muslim faith, and have developed a defensive bunker mentality toward Islam. Some of these folks nurture attitudes that could careen out of control, becoming deep and explosive hatreds. It is vital that Christians learn how to live side-by-side with growing Islamic communities, to be friends but without sacrificing our distinctions. One of the tragedies of some of the more ecumenical incarnations of the Christian faith found predominantly in the mainline churches is that they tend to be all too willing to surrender their specifics in the name of good relationships.

I learned a lot one evening several years ago as I listened to a lecture being delivered by Bishop Kenneth Cragg, one of the Anglican Church's leading Islamic scholars, a man who spent most of his active ministry in the Middle East. His love for Islam and the Muslim people shone through as he spoke in a winsome manner to a smallish group on the campus of a well-known university in Virginia. At the end of his presentation, one of the students asked him a perceptive question. If he was so enthusiastic about Islam, why was he not a Muslim.

This was the opportunity for the bishop to tell the gathering of his own encounter with Jesus Christ. "We need to see the situation in redemptive terms," he said. "For all its magnificence, there is no crown of thorns in Islam—Christianity says there's a vicariousness in the heart of God, and we see the vulnerability of God in Jesus Christ. I would not have known what to make of the world had it not been for the Cross of Christ." Kenneth Cragg did a lot to help me rethink and temper my own attitudes toward Islam. How many times I have pondered his wise words that we need always to be watchful if we think we have divine warrant to undertake unholy acts or nurture unholy thoughts.

One of the great questions of the twenty-first century, as yet unanswered, is whether we can maintain our Christian clarity while, at the same time, entering into something approaching fraternal relationships with our Islamic sisters and brothers—as well as those of other competing religious traditions, even if they are showing little fraternity toward us. This is going to require a capacity to live with ambiguity, something that most of us find hard because of a cultural yearning to see everything in terms of black and white.

We could find ourselves unexpected allies as we confront some of the issues that are careening down the pike toward us. All theists, for example, work from similar bases when it comes to the manner in which we approach the ethical issues raised by bioscientific advance, even if we disagree fundamentally about the person and importance of Jesus Christ. Can we make practical alliances to counter the dark underside of human discovery, while at the same time holding competing views on the source of redemption? The jury is still out on such questions— but now is the time to be testing the waters.[13]

### It's Formation, Stupid!

Do you remember the words that James Carville had over his desk as he managed Bill Clinton's successful bid for the presidency in 1992: "It's the economy, stupid!" Looking at the challenge that is before us as we move into a new century, I would want us to change the word *economy* to *formation*. One of the primary tasks before us is to form people in Christ. We have been very poor in the mainline churches at making disciples, and addressing this has to be high on our agendas.

As I monitor the development of this unexpected spirituality boom, it appears to be so rich with God-given opportunities for Christian ministry that it is hard to know where to begin, yet there are few congregations that are really taking advantage of these extraordinary circumstances. One reason for this is that Christians have such a shallow commitment to and understanding of their faith that they do not know how to grasp what is going on. They have such little confidence in their own spiritual tradition that the churches have been slow to see how this increased consciousness of the unseen world might be an ally in mission and ministry.

One of the enduring criticisms of so many spiritual searchers is that as they look at the churches they do not see Christians living out a spirituality of any kind. While their criticisms might be overstated, colored by a sense that Christianity is irrelevant and "old hat," we need to listen and take seriously what they are saying. Philosopher and pastor Dallas Willard writes that those on every side of the debates that fracture the churches do not lay "down a coherent framework of knowledge and practical direction adequate to personal transformation toward the abundance and obedience emphasized in the New Testament, with a corresponding redemption of ordinary life. What is taught as the essential message about Jesus has no natural connection to entering a life of discipleship to him."[14]

Willard's observation, which can be repeated over and over again, cuts to the quick of the shallowness of American Christian life and experience. I wish I had a dollar for every time someone said that American Christianity tends to be a mile wide and an inch deep. Knowing Jesus is just not enough; deepening roots in Jesus has to be a priority of the churches as we enter this new century for the renewal of heart and mind will, when properly formed, overflow into life and lifestyle. As wonderful a tool as the Alpha Course might be, getting people to a commitment to faith in Christ is only the beginning. What follows is the hard, hard work of turning that commitment into obedience. I find it encouraging that the Episcopal Diocese of Milwaukee, under the leadership of Bishop Roger White, is working to revamp its catechetical process, in place for more than a dozen years, so that it provides the beginnings of a decent follow-through for Alpha, which is being used by a score or more congregations in the diocese. Others are working in a similar direction.

What is worrying about this spiritual change within the heart of the culture is that even those Christians who are willing to explore the possibilities of the spirituality explosion seem to downplay the extraordinary riches of their own spiritual traditions, flirting with a whole variety of others at their expense. An example of this is the *Spirituality Today* journal that has been published with significant support from Trinity Church, Wall Street. One has to carefully peruse the pages, at least of the earlier issues, to find any positive affirmation of Christian spiritual values at all. Meanwhile, they are all over folks like the Dalai Lama and self-help gurus like Thomas Moore. This is not to cast aspersions at either of these two eminent gentlemen, their spiritual insights, or their supporters, but it does illustrate how embarrassed so many of us seem to be by the treasures we seem to want to keep locked in a dark, damp corner of the church's basement.

Eric Major, who heads up the religious publishing program of Doubleday, has suggested that with the passing of the millennium, "the religious fervor will quiet down. It's been at such a high pitch for so long that it can't maintain such a high level, and I see a much quieter faith emerging." From his perch in the publishing world, he sees a growing hunger for the richness offered by the liturgy. "Traditional churches are finding more people structuring their faith," he comments—which means drawing upon the treasures accumulated from the past.[15]

As far as spirituality and the Episcopal Church are concerned, for example, it is paradoxical that as more and more people are rooting and grounding themselves in a richer and more substantial tradition, we have been so deliberately cavalier with our own historic and liturgical treasures, tossing them aside in favor of balloons and banalities.[16] As the spirituality movement reaches toward some kind of maturity, it provides one of the most magnificent opportunities for literally centuries for parishes to reach out to these spiritual travelers who want to put flesh on the bones of believing. This should be gleefully seized and "exploited" to the fullest.

This fresh infusion of spiritual consciousness into the culture presents us with an enormous challenge and opportunity. Let me repeat once again that it means, among other things, that we should be working hard on issues of Christian formation. We should also be finding ways to minister effectively to those whose appetite for things spiritual has been awakened through some kind of sectary or strange religious group. Such folks are starting to appear at church doors. The problem is that the churches do not look particularly appetizing to them, or all that spiritual. Retreats, teaching in spiritual disciplines, schools of prayer, Web sites, and a thousand other tools are there, waiting for us to dust them off and put them to use in the service of the Gospel.

One of the questions that future historians are likely to ask when they look back on the church's response to this spiritual awakening, for that is what it is, is how we capitalized upon the opportunities. If we remain caught up in our own little ecclesiastical world, we are likely to be given failing grades.

✦ ✦ ✦

## To Think and Talk Over

1. Why do secular people find it so difficult to believe that the Christian faith has anything to do with spirituality?
2. Discuss some of the consequences that might result from science increasingly affirming the existence of a creative divine hand rather than denying the existence of such an intelligent being.
3. How much Postmodern talk about spirituality is self-centered, and how much of it is a real searching after a relationship with a divinity of some kind?
4. Why do you think spirituality and small groups seem to go hand-in-hand with one another?
5. Is it alarmist to talk about the possibility of violent religious conflicts?
6. Why do you think it is that churches are so frightened or so incapable of deeply forming people in their faith in Jesus Christ?

## Suggestions on Further Reading

Foster, Richard. *Streams of Living Water—Celebrating the Great Traditions of Christian Faith* (San Francisco: HarperSanFrancisco, 1998).

Gallup, George H., Jr., and Jones, Timothy. *The Next American Spirituality* (Colorado Springs, CO: Cook Communications, 2000).

Gallup, George H., Jr., and Jones, Timothy. *The Saints Among Us* (Harrisburg, PA: Morehouse Publications, 1992).

Howard, Michael. *God in the Depths* (London: SPCK, 1999).

McGrath, Alister. *Roots That Refresh* (London: Hodder and Stoughton, 1991).

Peterson, Eugene H. *Subversive Spirituality* (Grand Rapids, MI: Wm. B. Eerdmans Publishing Co., and Regent College, 1994, 1997).

Popcorn, Faith. *Clicking* (New York: HarperCollins, 1996).

Willard, Dallas. *The Divine Conspiracy* (San Francisco: HarperSanFrancisco, 1998).

Wright, N. T. *Bringing the Church to the World* (Minneapolis: Bethany House Publishers, 1992).

## Web Sites

- If you want a site that will give you links to just about every Christian spirituality Web site imaginable, then I would suggest you peruse *Lift Up Your Hearts*, the Christian spirituality Web site of the Evangelical Lutheran Church in Canada. It can be reached at www.worship.on.ca/map.html.

- Another compendium of spirituality resources can be found at the library Web site of the Graduate Theological Union in Berkley, California. The site can be found at www.gtu.edu/library/LibSpirit.html.
- Interested in doing a master's degree in Christian spirituality? Then Sarum College, Salisbury, England, in association with the University of Wales, Lampeter, is a place to think of studying: www.sarum.ac.uk.
- For details of the research into spirituality being undertaken by George Gallup, Jr., and the Princeton Religion Research Center that he leads, go to www.prrc.org. At this Web site you will find details of the *Emerging Trends* newsletter that George Gallup puts together each month.
- Beliefnet is a Web site that deals with all things religious from all traditions, with one particular area of focus being spirituality. Its address is www.beliefnet.com.
- The Episcopal Church's weekly, *The Living Church*, has just launched a spirituality Web site for younger Christians who are Web savvy. The address is www.faithlinks.org.

# TREND NINE
# Learning to Live with and Love the Internet

*As we interconnect ourselves, many of the values of a nation state will give way to those of both larger and smaller electronic communities. We will socialize in digital neighborhoods in which physical space will be irrelevant and time will play a different role.*[1]

Nicholas Negroponte, Director, MIT, Media Lab

### The Internet Crept Up and Caught Us by Surprise

The Internet is a world-changing entity that has arrived on the scene in earnest since Bishop Roger White and I wrote *New Millennium, New Church* a decade ago, turning everything upside down. That the pair of us did not foresee the speed with which it would arrive, or the influence that it would exert, should surprise none of us—with all the dollars and resources that he has at his disposal, Bill Gates of Microsoft missed this one as well until it was almost too late!

What is amazing is that only a dozen years ago the Internet, originally a child of the U.S. military, was basically the preserve of "nerds," computer "jocks," and research scientists, not the bustling driver of the economy that it is in the process of becoming today. Less than ten years ago I was part of a demonstration of e-mail and online communication at a global mission conference. While one or two of the group gathered around the computer saw the possibilities that the technology offered, most were puzzled that we would waste their time with something so dull and esoteric! Oh, how the world has changed. This is a great tool for global mission—already today I have received e-mails from four different countries in various parts of the world, and that is less than average!

When talking about the role that the Internet is playing (and is going to play) in the process of globalization, there are probably not enough superlatives to go around. The Net is changing the way we handle both time and distance. "Distance means less and less in the digital world. In fact, an Internet user is utterly oblivious to it," writes digital communications pioneer Nicholas Negroponte. "On the Internet, distance often seems to function in reverse. I frequently get faster replies from distant places than close ones because the time change allows people to answer while I sleep—so it feels closer."[2]

This same phenomenon comes into play when we enter the world of online business, or, as it has become known, e-commerce. Anyone launching any endeavor on the Net these days is immediately setting up as an international business. In theory, at least, the mom-and-pop enterprise that is run off the kitchen table has the same global reach as Wal-Mart, Microsoft, or Amazon.com. I have found it much more convenient to do the bulk of my shopping online than to go trailing off around the mall, especially at Christmastime. In addition, I am now able to make purchases from vendors all over the world due to the Internet.[3]

Furthermore, this international electronic approach to life cannot help but reach its tentacles into almost every other facet of our lives influencing everything, including our ecclesiastical configurations. Churches can no longer organize themselves and function oblivious to electronic communities any more than can businesses, cities, or nations, yet in many facets of the life of the mainline denominations, this is exactly what we are trying to do. The problem is that when Christian organizations finally do decide to try to break into this new world being born, they do it so terribly badly. Excellence is a word that seems to be missing from so many of our vocabularies.

The Internet is making it inevitable that geography is only one of the dimensions that needs to be taken into account when we talk about mission, ministry, or church organization. It seems inevitable that while traditional judicatories that cover a contiguous area, for example, will not entirely disappear, there will also be some kind of overlay of non-geographical dioceses or conferences that affiliate with one another and the wider church more on the basis of affinity rather than proximity. Traditionalists may scream, but there is a fast emerging reality.

If you think this far fetched, then visit the Roman Catholic Diocese of Partenia at www.partenia.org. It is the brainchild of Jacque Gaillot, the former Bishop of Evreux in France. After falling foul of the Vatican in 1995, Gaillot was translated to the titular see of Partenia in Algeria. Once a bustling oasis, Partenia, on the slopes of the Atlas Mountains, is now deserted. But Bishop Gaillot turned it into the world's first virtual diocese, which he presides over from his home in Paris. It has become an Internet stopping-off point for his kind of Catholics. It is translated into half a dozen languages, including English, and visitors can enter into conversation with the bishop through his e-mail address. "Partenia is a fully empowered Catholic diocese. Through its web site, the church is extending its reach to thousands, potentially millions of people previously banned from its teachings by law or force of circumstances. Anywhere and anytime, anyone with net access can now learn something about Catholicism or about any other religion."[4]

This global communications network, of which easy air travel, cheap telephone calls, and the Internet are primary components, is in the process of reworking more of our hopes, dreams, and expectations than most of us realize. Geography is no longer the limiting factor that it once was—and if ecclesiastical boundaries are not sacrosanct, neither are national boundaries. This does not mean that the nationstate will disappear, but its role is being redesigned and reworked, and its power and autonomy are being greatly reduced by travel and digital interconnectedness, in addition to the global economy, already discussed.

Leading futurist John Naisbitt wrote several years ago that "e-mail is a tribe maker. Electronics makes us more tribal at the same time it globalizes us." He then goes on to say:

> Economic and technological forces of change have weakened the nationstate, but they have strengthened, not separated people from, long-standing identities. Language, culture, religion, and ethnic heritage reinforce people's sense of belonging. These are the bonds out of which will be created new communities.[5]

### By Trial and Error

Just as it took a long time for broadcasters to work out how television was different from radio in the sort of programming that it demanded, so right now we are in the midst of a huge process of experimentation as everyone from academics to art galleries works out how to use the Internet and these emerging digital communications effectively. Relatively few e-commercial ventures have yet discovered how to use the Internet for a profit; the year 2000 saw scores of ambitious dot.com companies biting the dust. Not even the media companies with their tremendous resources and expertise have yet discovered how to use the Internet to make money.

One of the reasons for this is that they have been experimenting with a variety of marketing techniques in conjunction with a technology that is still emerging. Until now the ability to communicate necessary quantities of data and information has been hampered by the scarcity of band width on the national and global telecommunications network. That is all changing as massive advances are being made in the field of optics, fiber optic cable, and satellite communications. While Moore's law states that computing power doubles every eighteen months, band width is increasing at least twice that rate. This means that the Internet is being turbo charged—and that the integration of the world and its markets could probably hardly have begun!

But, there are still many problems ahead. Purveyors of copyrighted materials, like words and music, are finding it extremely difficult to protect their asset from Napster and all sorts of Internet freeloaders. Even college professors who have used the Web to help them with their teaching are pulling their hair out that almost before they have distributed it, their teaching content is on student Web sites all over the place. More menacing is that we have not yet really learned how to protect this fragile medium from intrusion by hackers, pranksters, and serious cyberterrorists.

In both faith and commerce, some are having more success in this field than others. There are some mission-driven Christian units who are beginning to discover that there are all sorts of ways of making the Internet work for them and their ministries—although like even bigger fish in this pond, they have yet to resolve the issue of how properly to finance their online activities. Meanwhile, as this experimentation goes on, it is altering the way we relate to one another, to the economy, and to the world community.

Thomas L. Friedman, a leading columnist at *The New York Times,* talks about one of the most powerful influences shaping the world today as the Electronic Herd.

> The global marketplace today is an Electronic Herd of often anonymous stock, bond, currency and multinational investors, connected by screens and networks . . . The Electronic Herd cuts no one any slack. *No one.* It does not recognize anyone's unique circumstances. The herd knows only its own rules . . . Countries cannot thrive in today's world without plugging into the Elec-

tronic Herd, and they cannot survive unless they learn how to get the best out of this herd without being overwhelmed or shocked by its inevitable surges.[6]

What Friedman is trying to tell us, using rich imagery and colorful language, is that a very, very different era is dawning—and we ignore this reality at our own peril. What brought the ubiquitous power of digital communication home to me most clearly was the discovery that my prosperous and fanatically technophobic brother had started taking computer lessons. After years spent fighting the trend, he finally bought a PC for his desk and had got himself an e-mail address. The reason for this about turn is simple: If he does not have these things he will find it more difficult to continue making money!

While there are a few voices in both church and the wider culture that seem absolutely determined to pooh-pooh the revolutionary impact of the Internet, little doubt remains about its earth-shattering influence on the world. What is more, these forces that have been brought into play are reworking the landscape every six to eight months as the technology upgrades and more becomes possible. Quite frankly, most Christians, but especially creedal and orthodox Christians, have not been particularly effective in their use of the Internet to date, perhaps because they are not really interested. These are still relatively early days and that could (and should) change, but the longer we dither the more catching up will be involved. Many of those diverse religious groups that have sprung up, and about which we talked in the previous chapter, especially those whose ideals have a strong Gnostic style and flavor, have been much quicker off the mark.

### The Internet Changes the Way We Work

It has been estimated that by 2015 there could be as many as 100 million virtual migrant workers selling their skills through the Net. The arrival of cheap broadband communications technology is going to have radical unpleasantries. For example, men and women all over the world, instead of jumping into their cars or boarding a train or bus, are likely to log on in the mornings and go to work by Internet in a different time zone—or another country on the other side of the world. Already the world's financial markets are a twenty-four-hour-a-day phenomenon, and the Internet is used for trading on whatever market happens to be open for business at that point, and work is fast moving in that direction. The world's stock markets are responding to this phe-

nomenon and are building the kind of alliances that will enable them to
exploit these opportunities.

One Friday in early 1999 I found myself sitting with a group of men
in a hostelry in New England where they were winding down after a
long week. One of the guys there was a young businessman, the son of
an old friend. He had once been a student in my parish's Sunday school!
He had just quit a position at a major corporation and was working on
a business idea that would put him at the forefront of the digital revolution. It was his dream to broker the skills of Russian and Ukrainian
software engineers to companies in North America that are starved of
employees with such skills.

Alas, nothing came of his dream, but it demonstrated that it is possible with a little imagination and today's technology. It would have enabled Eastern Europeans to remain in their homelands, do
programming work for high tech companies in the Northeast—and
earn world-class salaries in the process. The equipment needed for such
an enterprise was already available, in place, and whereas a couple of
years earlier it would have cost an arm and a leg, at that point it was
coming within reach of a nimble and far-sighted small businessperson.

While the old-fashioned office is unlikely to disappear anytime
soon, more and more people are going to find themselves telecommut-
ing to work at least once or twice a week—if only to unclog the already
overloaded road system. Companies like Ford and Delta Airlines are
making it easy for their employees to acquire computers so that they are
electronically accessible and able to work from home occasionally. Now
that telecommunications costs have tumbled, it is possible for a
Chicago attorney to live in, say, Telluride, Colorado, because she loves
the mountains. Her receptionist/personal assistant might be a thousand miles away, but clients don't know that when they are put through
to her home office looking out across the mountains. Furthermore,
there is no reason why they should know that she is comfortably
dressed in her sweatsuit and bunny slippers! Of course, being in the office is no longer essential because she no longer needs access to a huge
library of legal works; she can do the necessary research for her briefs
on the Internet, possibly assisted by a paralegal whose home might be
somewhere else, like in San Diego, or Santiago, Chile.

By 2015, it is highly likely that increased computing power and
broadband information transfer will turn virtual reality from a dream
into a fact. It will enable a much more convincing and meaningful interface between employer and employee, consultant and consultee,
lover and beloved, even though they might be thousands of miles apart.

This is bound to make transcontinental work relationships much easier. Who knows, within a relative handful of years, being interviewed for a post could mean chatting to a foot-tall holographic projection of your potential boss who is an ocean and six time zones away. Professor Stephen Benton of the Spatial Imaging Group at M.I.T.'s Media Laboratory is working on the technology that will lead to holographic videoconferencing. He believes that "within the next ten to twenty years . . . it will be possible for a family whose members are scattered across the country to share a virtual Thanksgiving, say, clinking ethereal wineglasses through the void."[7]

Such sophisticated interconnection also has its downside. It is highly likely that by that time people will be using virtual reality as an entertainment "escape hatch." Given the volume of questionable and sexual traffic that is currently clogging the Internet, the possibilities that people are likely to be pursuing should not surprise anyone.

### Another Meeting Place

In coming years we can expect more and more commerce, retailing, and business to move into cyberspace, as well as education, facets of government, and certain health care functions. Increasingly, as the boundaries between traditional broadcasting and the Internet blur, we will go into cyberspace looking for more of our leisure and entertainment. The Millennial Generation, those born since the mid-eighties, already prefer the Net to television. Prime-time viewing will be whenever you want it, and you will be able to download a full-length movie from the provider in a few seconds. Furthermore, the Internet will be another major setting in which you develop friendships and relationships with people everywhere. This is already happening among the adolescent and pre-adolescent set. We can readily expect this to grow by leaps and bounds in the years ahead.

Some of us are already experiencing the possibilities in a rudimentary kind of way. Sometimes in the mornings I say "hi" to my good friend, the Reverend Canon Sarah Gaede at St. Luke's Episcopal Cathedral, Orlando, Florida, who is on my AOL Buddy List. Sarah's morning schedule seems to follow a similar routine to mine, which means that she is often online doing her e-mail at the same time as I am, and the software is set up in such a way to tell me that she is around—so off goes an instant message to her.

Then, a while back, when I was experiencing significant emotional and spiritual distress, I turned to Dave Macgregor for pastoral counsel.

There is nothing unusual in that, except that Dave, a retired cathedral dean who was born in New Zealand, lives in South Africa—and I have never actually met him face to face. As I poured out my soul into my online Instant Messenger, Dave fielded my anxieties, prayed for me, and ministered to my aching heart. There will be more and more exchanges similar to this in the years to come. There is enormous potential for pastoral ministry online, and we have yet even to begin grasping some of the opportunities.

In my perambulations around the Net over the last few years, I have had interesting instant-message conversations with computer geeks in Bangalore, India, teachers in Australia, as well as all sorts of folks in Germany, Britain, and South Africa. It won't be long before we will be able to see each other, talk rather than type, and so forth. I also have taught an online class that had twelve students of four nationalities, situated on three continents.

E-mail is now so ubiquitous that not only do I keep in contact with people all over the world in this way, but folks have now started, as a matter of course, giving me their e-mail address rather than their "snail mail" address or telephone number. This means that people who were once so far away that contact was difficult to maintain are now within easy chatting distance. Friendships that would have died can be maintained, and many of us have had the experience of reawakening relationships from years back because of the accessibility of the Internet.

When I write something that is published online and which interests people, before you can say "gigabyte," I am receiving comments upon it from individuals around the world who have had my words passed on to them and have been touched by what I have said. Recently, I reviewed a book written by a friend that had received somewhat limited publicity in Britain but had not sold one copy in the U.S.A. That review rapidly accelerated sales to such an extent on the western shores of the Atlantic that online booksellers had to back-order it! All I had done was post it to my listserv of 400 or so people, and it had gone on from there to a number of parts of the world, and to Christians in a variety of denominational traditions.

### English—The Lingua Franca

The Internet could also be in the process of changing the linguistic balance of the world. English, which had more than a head start before this cyberrevolution, is now firmly entrenching itself as the unofficial language of the world, because it is the nearest thing to the "official" language of the Web, much as it is the official language of global commercial aviation. More than this, it is the American version of the English language, written and spoken, that is coming to predominate.

When working on a potential publishing project with a team in Britain, we discussed which spellings and approach to punctuation we should use—Commonwealth or American? One of the team, a priest, journalist, writer, and former religious radio producer in Britain, insisted that we use the American spelling. When I asked him why, he pointed out that the Internet was so oriented toward the American style of spelling that standardization would inevitably go in that direction. "Within a generation," David Winter, the priest-journalist said, "I suspect that the British approach to spelling will be entirely eclipsed." We shall see.

This facet of the Internet offers fascinating evangelistic opportunities, but those of us in the Anglo world need to take great care that we do not stumble even further into cultural imperialism. One of the byproducts of this turn of events is that in the twenty-first century we are going to have to work hard to protect minority ethnic and linguistic groups, even as the electronic world encourages them to assert their individuality. It will be paramount that those of us in the prevailing cultures enable minority cultures and ethnicities to survive. It has to be remembered that one of the primary avenues through which culture is transmitted is language. As Christians, who honor such cultural and ethnic diversity, this is going to be an important task in this century.

### Change, Change, Change

It is my perception, backed up by the affirmation of others against whom I have tested this idea, that the advent of the Internet during the 1990s speeded up and is altering the metabolism of change. This global information superhighway has introduced us to the joys and perils of instant communication anywhere on the planet. This means ideas are spread and assimilated much more quickly than was previously the case.

Stephen Bertman, an American who teaches at Ontario's University of Windsor, has written convincingly about this whole phenomenon. "Ongoing technological advances have accelerated three types of activity in particular: the movement of things (through commerce), the movement of ideas (through communications), and the movement of people (through transportation). The combined acceleration of these separate but related activities has generated a swirling vortex that today sucks into itself all elements of individual experience, thought, and emotion."[8]

Nowhere is this vortex more apparent than in church life. Those who ten years ago were on a periphery have discovered how empowering the Internet can be. Many have become extremely skilled at using the Net—turning themselves overnight from spectators into players, especially in the organizational life of the churches. They have discovered how to use it to ensure that their views, theologies, orthodoxies, or heterodoxies are not overlooked. As helpful as this might be in certain respects, there has been at times a tendency for trivia to begin masquerading as meaning.

In the twenty-first century it is possible for ideas spawned yesterday in out-of-the-way places to be everywhere today, and be accepted as normative tomorrow. This has speeded the advance (or retreat) of ideas and the intensity of debate. It also means that the church is being democratized (and relativized) in such a way that now everyone can have a say in the pressing issues of the day, and not just those we elect to represent us at each level of ecclesiastical governance. The churning of the Internet is accelerating and will continue to ferment for a good while to come, especially as refinements of this communication technology continue to alter the way we relate to one another.

Stephen Bertman goes on to say:

> The age of communications is also paradoxically an age of vulnerability. In a society highly dependent upon communication, the individual is more than ever before susceptible to the quality of information he receives and, thus, can be more readily managed by others than in a society where less needs to be communicated. In short, our life comes down to this: We are what we are told and shown. For it is mostly from the data that we are presented with that we construct our mental pictures of reality. The questions a society asks will ultimately depend upon the reality it acknowledges. In short, before any problem can be addressed, people must first realize it exists.[9]

The cyberworld has its downside, for not only is its infrastructure extremely fragile, but it is increasingly being used by criminals for fraud. And it is not just Westerners who know how to rip one another off or steal information online. The last trip that I made to

Russia was in 1998, and I was unable to log onto the Internet as I had done on previous visits. Infuriating as this might have been, the reason was simple: My Internet service provider (ISP) had temporarily withdrawn service on discovering that it was being used by the mafia for illegal activities, so that it could create electronic firewalls to protect itself.

Pornographers discovered very rapidly how to ply their wares on the Net—becoming among the first business-to-customer operations to become profitable in e-commerce. The Internet is, at the moment, replete with a frightening unwholesomeness. Vast quantities of salacious material being peddled with a sophistication that far exceeds anything being used by the religious, educators, medics, or others with a more worthwhile message to share. I read a commentator in a computer magazine who suggested marketers should go to school on the methods being pioneered by porn merchants!

If, as we have seen, society had trouble adjusting to television when it came rumbling into prominence during the 1940s and 1950s, adjusting to this new medium with the legion of possibilities that accompany it is putting even more of a strain on our existing systems. The Internet, in all its glory (and otherwise), is providing Christian people with challenges the likes of which they have never known before—and these challenges are not going to go away anytime soon. What puzzles me is how few people are taking this seriously. I think one reason for this is the false notion that technology is somehow morally neutral, when this really is not so.

✦ ✦ ✦

## To Think and Talk Over

1. Think and talk about the difference the Internet has made in your life. If it has made no difference at all, ask yourself why that is.
2. Does it trouble you that the Internet is changing our relationship with geography and distance? If so, why?
3. If the Internet has brought together "electronic tribes," what impact do you think such groups can have on the way we live our lives?
4. How can Christians use the Internet as a meeting place?
5. Is it a bad thing that the American brand of English is becoming the predominant language of the world?
6. Discuss whether technology is morally neutral.
7. Is too much change a bad thing?

**Suggestions for Further Reading**

Bertman, Stephen. *Hyperculture* (Westpoint, CT: Praeger, 1998).
Friedman, Thomas L. *The Lexus and the Olive Tree* (New York: Farrar, Straus, Giroux,1999).
Gilder, George. *Telecosm: How Infinite Band Width Will Revolutionize Our World* (New Youk: Fortress Press, 2000).
Naisbitt, John. *Global Paradox* (New York: William Morrow & Company, 1994).
Negroponte, Nicholas. *Being Digital* (London: Hodder and Stoughton, 1995).
*Wired* magazine
*Christianity On-line* magazine

**Web Sites**

- Perhaps one of the most successful Christian Web presences is that of Christianity On-line—part of the *Christianity Today* stable of companies. It can be reached at www.ChristianityOn-line.com, or at AOL Keyword "CO."
- Anglicans On-line is probably the most extensive Anglican Web presence. It can be found at www.anglicansonline.org.
- Many conservative and evangelical Anglican ministries can be found at www.episcopalian.org.
- Discovering Ancient Wisdom at www.discovering-wisdom.com/ is an excellent example of Postmodern Web evangelism, sponsored by the International Bible Society. This Web site reaches out to the Postmodern generations as they hunger for ancient truths, mysticism, and spirituality. The Web site presents Scripture from the Gospels and from the wisdom books of Job, Proverbs and Ecclesiastes in a fresh way. Its format is designed to reach people who aren't necessarily looking for the Bible.
- An excellent example of an informative Web site is that of the Alpha Course, which is at www.alpha.org.uk or www.alphana.org.

# TREND TEN
# Massive Theological Rethinking

*We now live in a transitional time in which the modern worldview of the Enlightenment is crumbling and a new worldview is beginning to take shape. Some leaders will insist on preserving the Christian faith in its Modern form; others will run headlong into the sweeping changes that accommodate Christianity to Postmodern forms; and a third group will carefully and cautiously seek to interface historic Christian truths into the dawning of a new era.*[1]

Robert E. Webber, theologian and college professor

### Theology Responds to the Changing Culture

The previous nine trends that we have been looking at are fairly easy to deduce if you are trying to keep a finger on the pulse of the emerging culture. Some, like globalization, for instance, jump out and bite you on the bottom—there is no way of escaping them! However, this final trend may be a little harder to pin down. There are profound pressures shaping it, but I also think it is still very much in embryonic form. Of all the trends identified, this is the one whose blossoming is the most difficult to foresee.

My hunch is that if (or when) this happens, it will come in with a long, slow burn, rather than a sudden burst from the heavens, because it will reflect the manner in which minds are slowly changed by altering circumstances and intellectual movements. Given the observations made thus far, this is a trend that will have the profoundest long-term impact on the world and the worldwide Christian family, but we may not necessarily see the manner in which it works itself out for several decades.

Of all the trends we have looked at in this book, theological rethinking is the one with the least certainty, but my instinct tells me it is beginning to happen. Small, out-of-the-way indicators confirm the reality of massive theological rethinking—like a story in the monthly newsletter *Religion Watch*, quoting the magazine *Lingua Franca* as it looks at the way evangelicalism is dealing with the rise of Postmodernity. The piece wonders if "in the attempt to understand and appropriate the highly influential movement known as Postmodernism, several well-known evangelical scholars have ventured into intellectual territory that has proven highly controversial and, to some, worrisome about evangelicalism's future."

Evangelical four-year colleges have managed to maintain their firm theological stance for a number of decades, shored up by warnings that if they do not they might go down the same path taken by the mainline Protestant universities and colleges during the last century, as they succumbed to secularization. "Noted for its suspicions, even rejection of universal truths, master narratives, Scriptural authority, and prepositional normative truth, Postmodernism is now being studied carefully by a variety of evangelical scholars."[2] And, it seems, as these scholars attempt to understand the faith within this emerging culturing context they are challenging some of the long-accepted canons of evangelical belief.

Evangelicals, like Christians of various other theological flavors, are clearly wrestling to make sense of the radical change that is reshaping the intellectual and worldview climates of our culture. The seeds of these trends were planted long ago, but it has only been in the last ten to fifteen years that they have really burgeoned. Graham Cray, Principal of Ridley Hall, one of the Church of England's seminaries in Cambridge, follows in the footsteps of a host of other observers who have affirmed that this is a "hinge" moment in history, and that Generation X, those born between the early-sixties and the mid-eighties, is the "hinge" generation—the first to be truly influenced by a massive cultural shift that is taking place.

> Western culture is undergoing a fundamental shift. It is both a shift in the shape and organization of society and the way people find their identity within it (Postmodernity) and in the paradigm or worldview by which people make sense of society and make their decisions within it (Postmodernism) . . . The central

question to be faced is how should we respond to the emerging culture in a way which is true to the gospel. In every era and society the Christian Church faces the challenge of contextualization—ensuring that the gospel is being relevantly addressed to its culture from within, while avoiding syncretism—the cultural context being allowed to shape the gospel to such an extent that its costly or prophetic challenge to individuals and to society is neutralized.[3]

As this major transition continues, churning up the bedrock and pushing aside the vast majority of Judeo-Christian values, Western believers are for the first time in approximately seventy generations being challenged to live in a culture that has cast itself adrift from the predominance of Christian ideas and values. Postmodernity is the name given to an array of ideas that have yet to really congeal, but ideas that are emerging from the decay of the Modern, industrial world of the Enlightenment. Suspicious of absolutes and rejecting virtually all notions of universal truth, master narratives, and the ultimate authority of Scripture, it provides an ideal environment in which today's multicultural pluralism can thrive. Postmodernity is virulent, but it may only be a transitional intellectual phase while we are on our way to something else.

### What Goes Around, Comes Around

History has come full circle, and we now are back in world that bears certain striking resemblances to the one into which Jesus Christ was born, and from which a Christian faith has grown. If there is to be any sort of Christendom in the future—which I rather doubt—it is more likely to come to fruition in Africa or Latin America than the pluralistic, secular-pagan West. Although, it is true to say that electronic communications means that no culture will ever again be able to develop in isolation from other cultures, faiths, and belief systems. So, whether they like it or not, Postmodernity will be a challenge even in those places where the church now appears to be riding high and reaping extraordinary harvests.

The truth is that in the West we now do our believing in a missionary situation rather than as members of a society that is at its heart tolerant or even congenial to our creeds and ideals. While there continue to be large numbers of Christians in the developed world, the influence that the faith once had over the culture is waning rapidly, and too many of those who are believers are more in tune with the values of the culture than the essence of the Christian worldview. This means that wherever we are on the theological spectrum, we are being driven back to reconsider what it is to be Christian, to look afresh at the classical Christian tradition of the first five centuries of the church's life, and to examine how its notions speak to the emerging present and fast-approaching future.

The Canadian Baptist thinker and pastor Alan J. Roxburgh laments the fact that the church's leadership is not intellectually equipped to handle such a challenge but is primarily made up of technicians. These folks are, he contends, "mechanics of the latest method offering two hundred, surefire, guaranteed-to-work ways of making your congregation the most alive, fastest-growing, seeker-sensitive, liturgical, charismatic church in North America." These individuals "are not qualified to chart the course ahead for the church."[4]

If we examine closely the development of certain strands of thought within the mainline traditions during the tail-end of the nineteenth century and the first decades of the twentieth, we find ourselves looking at circumstances that bear a striking resemblance to those that currently face us. Those decades were a period when in the West the secularizing values of the Enlightenment were carrying all before them, and it was clear that conservative, creedal, orthodox Christianity was in eclipse—despite churches in many parts of Europe and North America that were bursting at the seams, and a huge procession of missionaries determined to bring about the "Evangelization of the World in Our Generation."

Theological liberalism, which rose to the surface during the latter part of the nineteenth century, seemed during those years of high Modernity to be unassailable, with conservative and orthodox believers forced into defensive positions as wave after wave of new ideas came along challenging the old verities. On either side of the Atlantic, conservatives backed themselves into all sorts of theological cul-de-sacs. Their scholarship was poor, their attitudes were aggressively defensive and reactionary, and many of their number were fixated on quirky peripheral issues rather than what was substantial. However, despite all this, what marked them out was their obvious piety and their commitment to mission and evangelism.

All this meant that while the intellectual foundations of their traditions floundered back at home, these were the folk planting new churches around the world. Their star might have been waning for a time in the Global North, but they were playing a disproportionate role in nurturing the Gospel in the Global South. The work they did during those years is now coming to fruition as we look at the size and the boundless energy of the churches they played a role in establishing. While the intellectual record of conservatives during that period leaves a lot to be desired in most instances, the fruit of their missionary zeal is bound to have an ever-more significant impact on the twenty-first century now that those more recently planted churches have reached maturity, and are taking leader-ship of the Christian project around the world.[5]

The intellectual state of conservatives, for example, during the mid-dle part of the twentieth century is pointed up in Timothy Dudley-Smith's biography of the noted English Anglican evangelical leader John Stott. He writes that whenever an evangelical Christian studied theology in a British university in the 1940s and managed to survive with convictions about divine revelation and the nature of salvation in-tact, it was considered a miracle—and that John Stott did just this. Speaking of Douglas Johnson, one of the leaders of evangelical student activity in British universities at that time, Bishop Dudley-Smith writes that "he had a clear conviction that pietism was not enough, but that an evangelical faith, if it was to be a vital force in the modern world, must be equipped to win the intellectual battles . . ."[6] What was true in Britain was also the case on the western side of the Atlantic Ocean, and parallel movements of evangelical intellectual renewal took place in mid-cen-tury in Anglo-Saxon communities on either side of the Atlantic, and in the Pacific.

In the years following World War II the worm slowly began to turn, but even into the 1970s evangelicals and those of conservative convic-tion were regarded as intellectual lightweights, hardly worthy of serious attention in both Europe and North America. Oxford theologian Alis-ter McGrath believes that 1977 probably represented the high water mark of classic theological liberalism in England, but that decline set in rapidly after that.[7] This is illustrated by how few theological conserva-tives held positions of leadership in the Western mainline churches, and how little credence was given to their beliefs. In the Episcopal Church in the U.S.A., even in the late 1970s, those who identified themselves with charismatic renewal often found themselves up against all sorts of pres-sures, while all those clergy who identified themselves as evangelicals could be fitted comfortably into a modest church hall—I know, I was one of them!

Yet something was happening. Seeds planted in the 1940s and 1950s were sprouting, conservative Christianity was growing, new believers were being converted to Christ from secular and post-

Christian backgrounds, the level of scholarship was rising, and all
these things brought with them new intellectual infusions. One of
the straws in the wind of this changing climate was the emergence of
what might best be called the "born again" phenomenon, picked up
aggressively by the American press in the mid-seventies when Jimmy
Carter started running for the presidency. Another straw is more
personal. In the second half of the sixties virtually no one in my seminary class in what was then the largest Anglican seminary in England had been raised in an overtly Christian home—I would
estimate that as many as 80 percent of us were from essentially nominal or unchurched backgrounds. This illustrates that a whole fresh
strain of leadership with perceptions from beyond the "ghetto" were
going to influence the future.

### The Changing Face and Influence of Liberal Christianity

Meanwhile, as biblical orthodoxy started to grow, classic devout liberal
Christianity (although politically still strong) was in numerical and intellectual decline. During the final third of the twentieth century we
have watched those on the leftward edge of the spectrum loosen their
hold on the creedal anchor and as a result their tradition has dissipated
its theological capital, which means there is less and less to transfer to
the following generations. Leander Keck, Dean Emeritus of Yale Divinity School, wrote that those churches who have taken this route, "despite their ample theological heritage, are no longer seriously teaching
the theological substance of the Christian faith."[8]

Keck goes on to say that in the teaching institutions of the majority
of mainline churches, anthropology has replaced theology, "class action" legalism has replaced the grace of the Gospel, and positive
hermeneutics have been replaced by a hermeneutic of suspicion and
even total alienation from the biblical text. Now that we are several generations into this trend, he points out, this is having a cumulatively
deleterious effect on the churches and congregations that are led by
clergy formed in this tradition.

Some of those at the more militant end of the liberal spectrum have,
in effect, abandoned Christianity altogether, creating from their own
imaginations a patchwork set of radical alternatives that seem so bent
on so revisioning the faith in their own image that it has reached a point
where substantial facets of their belief system bear only a vague passing
resemblance to the historic Christian tradition. For example, a leading
feminist/womanist theologian is reported to have described her female

colleagues as the church's "theological garbage collectors," because "someone's got to take out the trash." By this she means getting rid of much of the substance that Christians have believed for 2000 years, completely reworking the faith, and the language with which that faith is expressed. Such attitudes are more of an attack than a helpful contribution to serious intellectual discourse.

Even to the most generous soul in the world, it is increasingly difficult for creedal believers to affirm as Christians those who are at the extreme ends of the continuum, especially when bishops deny theism and supposedly serious theologians make statements like the ones I have just drawn attention to. It is hard to see where so much of this religious speculation might be leading, except eventually out of the Christian faith altogether, and maybe toward a syncretistic religion that might ring bells with certain fanciful components of the undefined and fuzzy "spirituality" that is in the Postmodern "ether."

Writing of the environment out of which all this has come, United Methodist theologian Tom Oden from Drew University in Madison, New Jersey, has said, "Not only is there no concept of heresy, but also there is no way even to raise the question of where the boundaries of legitimate Christian belief lie, when absolute relativism holds sway."⁹ As if to illustrate Oden's point, John Shelby Spong wrote that during his time as Episcopal Bishop of Newark, "I became increasingly committed to fashioning a diocese that allowed our clergy the freedom to risk, the ability to envision the future, and the capacity to experiment with liturgy, theology, and ecclesiology. My goal and my vocation was to open doors through which some people could make the transition into the future of our faith story."¹⁰ The tragedy of such open-endedness is that it rung very few bells with the people of the New Jersey suburbs that Spong thought he was communicating to, and the statistics of the Episcopal Diocese of Newark illustrate a decline.

In certain places it is likely that such views might prevail, and in what is tantamount to an act of piracy, those who hold them are likely to temporarily take over traditional church structures. The question is whether such belief systems have the capacity to sustain themselves from generation to generation. In other places, it seems likely that they will merge with some of the multiplicity of religious expressions in this pluralistic, Postmodern culture, creating a whole new array of gnostic hybrids—much as happened in the early centuries of Christian believing. And in other circumstances, they will probably lead away from believing altogether and get lost in the sea of secularity that washes around us.

Yet it may be encouraging to ponder the rather startling observation
made by Dutch missiologist Hans Hoekendijk and quoted several years
ago by Wilbert R. Shenk, a Mennonite who teaches at Fuller Theological Seminary. He said, "A church is authentic when (1) it has developed
its own way of sharing its faith in Jesus with other people, (2) it is com-
posing and singing its own songs, (3) it conducts its ecclesial life in a
culturally appropriate, rather than exotic, manner, and (4) it manages
to spawn a heresy or two!"[11]

## Postmodernity—Again

Yet this whole gamut of theological reflection that we have inherited
was profoundly shaped by now fast-departing Modernity. Whether we
are conservative, liberal, radical, or somewhere in between, those of us
over the age of forty have been doing our thinking and believing in an
environment thoroughly drenched by the principles of the Enlightenment. The notion that reason triumphs over all things, which is at the
heart of Enlightenment thinking, is at the very root of our perceptions.
But the Enlightenment, and the Modernity that it parented, is waning
fast, its place being taken by this slithery and difficult-to-define mindset known as Postmodernity.

Postmodernity is so hard to characterize that being amorphous
seems to be its predominant style. "There is no attendant clarity about
the *meaning* of (Postmodernism's) terminology. There are probably a
thousand different self-appointed commentators on the Postmodern
phenomenon and bewildering discrepancies between the ways many of
these authors understand the term *Postmodern* and its cognates."[12]
Some even wonder whether Postmodernity is a genuine intellectual
movement.

The varieties of Postmodernity do not create a cultural setting that
has a lot of patience with the modes of conception that the Enlightenment or creedal Christians have often prized. Postmodern people are
suspicious of what they conceive to be the heartless rationality of the
Enlightenment, and give a lot more credence than Modern people to
sensing, the spiritual, intuition, and unseen dimensions. Thus a new
component is being added to the Western theological process that cannot be ignored. The general population is starting to perceive reality
very differently under the tutelage of a barrage of relativistic ways of
thinking, and, as we have seen, the continuing advance of the sciences
themselves is forcing those on the cutting edge to step back from yesterday's hard-line positivism. The deep flaws of the Enlightenment,

flaws that have shaped the secularism of our world and burrowed their way into the theologizing of the churches, are now being revealed for the shortcomings that they are.

An entirely different kind of cultural milieu is being born. Its tentacles are already reaching into the Christian community, and it will inevitably influence more and more the way the church does its theology. I have noticed that younger Christians tend to approach their faith somewhat differently than their elders and many of the clergy, whose education in seminary taught them to answer Enlightenment-era questions that no one is asking anymore. They also deal with controversy in a totally different style.

As Christianity continues to lose its privileged position in this more spiritually sensitive world, our theological analysis will increasingly have to take into account the contradictory claims and worldviews that are all around us. In this process, experience will be as important as reason, if not more so. There is little doubt that we are moving back to a kind of environment that is strangely parallel to the first three or four centuries of Christian believing, where the church found it necessary to define what it believed against a panoramic backdrop of challenging religious and philosophical ideologies.

### The Wild Card of the Global South

Yet there is a further wild card thrown into play as a result of the influence of globalization. During the 1990s we watched the acceleration of the Western church's loss of predominance in the worldwide Christian family. No longer are those of us in Europe and North America the leaders of the global Christian family: that privilege and responsibility now falls upon the shoulders of the churches in the Global South. This being the case, it is going to be Africans, Asians, and Latin Americans who take the lead in shaping tomorrow's theological response to the surrounding reality—and we are going to have to get used to this fact.

While in the past when information moved more slowly it might have taken several generations for the ideas of these churches to percolate their way through to the lives of churches elsewhere in the world, this is no longer the case. Instant worldwide communications mean that they are already not just talking forcefully to us, but in many cases putting us on notice that yesterday's intellectual and spiritual configurations just will not do. Further advances in communications in the next ten years will mean that we can expect far greater involvement by thinkers from elsewhere in what we have considered our internal debates to this point. Indeed, within a generation we can fully expect that the intellectual and theological agendas of churches in the Global South will be the preeminent ones in the global Christian community, with those of us in the older churches sitting respectfully at their feet.

How all this will pan out is almost impossible to say, because so much deconstruction and reconstruction is being done all at once that it is hard to see many features of the landscape for all the dust that is being thrown up. It is also difficult to see how quickly some of the facets of the developing situation that I have identified will have their impact. However, what I can say is that during the first part of the twenty-first century we can fully expect a significant theological revolution to take place. It should be the hope and prayer of every single one of us that the new century will raise up the thinkers who have the capacity to lead us out of our present becalmed state and into something fresh and exciting—but something that is rooted in our Christian tradition, rather than riding roughshod over it.

✦ ✦ ✦

## To Think and Talk Over

1. Why is the reshaping of theology likely to have the profoundest impact of all upon the life of the churches?
2. What are likely to be the priorities of a church that lives in a missionary environment where the culture is neutral or hostile rather than friendly? How is this going to influence the way we live and the way we believe?
3. What evidence is there that the mainline churches have squandered their theological heritage, as Leander Keck believes?
4. So, when the church is renewed it spawns a heresy or two—what do you think of that idea?
5. What is it going to mean for the church to be living in a relativistic culture where every belief system is considered as valid as every other?
6. What influence do you think the churches in the Global South are likely to bring to bear upon the churches in the Global North?

## Suggestions for Further Reading

Blamires, Harry. *The Post-Christian Mind* (Ann Arbor, MI: Vine Books, 1999).
Carrell, Brian. *Moving Between Times* (Auckland, New Zealand: Deep Sight, 1998).

Keck, Leander. *The Church Confident* (Nashville, TN: Abingdon Press, 1994).

Lakeland, Paul. *Postmodernism—Christian Identity in a Fragmented Age* (Minneapolis, MN: Fortress Press, 1997).

McGrath, Alister. *A Passion for Truth: The Intellectual Coherence of Evangelicalism* (Downen Grove, IL: Inter-Varsity Press, 1996).

Oden, Thomas C. *Requiem—A Lament in Three Movements* (Nashville, TN: Abingdon Press, 1995).

Sweet, Leonard, *SoulTsunami* (Grand Rapids, MI: Zondervan, 1999).

Webber, Robert E. *Ancient-Future Faith* (Grand Rapids, MI: Baker Book House, 1999).

Wells, David F. *No Place for Truth* (Grand Rapids, MI: Wm. B. Eerdmans Publishing Co., 1993).

Wells, David F. *God in the Wasteland* (Grand Rapids, MI: Wm. B. Eerdmans Publishing Co., 1994).

Wells, David F. *Losing Our Virtue* (Grand Rapids, MI: Wm. B. Eerdmans Publishing Co., 1998).

### Web Sites

- One of the greatest theologians of our time, who gave a tremendous amount of thought to the manner in which Christian belief interfaces with the present, was the late Bishop Lesslie Newbigin. A complete bibliography of Bishop Newbigin's work can be found at www.deepsight.org/bibliog/newalpha.htm.

- There is an enormous amount of material about how evangelical theology is developing on www.ChristianityToday.com. This flagship publication of evangelical Christians has a majority of its 1990s issues online and accessible. They track the way evangelical theology is changing very well. I would particularly look at the issues from February 22, 2000; October, 25, 1999; February 8, 1999; October 6, 1997; August 11, 1997, just for starters.

- Since the beginning of 1997, I have moderated the Toward2015 listserv. It is a conversation about the future of our mission and ministry, and the challenges that face us. The archives of the conversations, which contain many fruitful interchanges (and some not so fruitful ones) can be accessed at listserv.episcopalian.org. If you wish to join the Toward2015 conversation, you can get on board there, too!

# CONCLUSION
# Why Trends?

*There are two elements that comprise a clear vision: the hope of the Gospel (what ought to be) and a significant understanding of a particular mission context (what is) . . . Any efforts at revisioning the church must evidence deep understanding of both these elements. This challenge is germane to the full spectrum of the institutional church, from local congregation to national denominations. All must revision themselves, and that vision must emerge out of a clear understanding of the grand story and our particular environment. Without such a vision, we wander—aimlessly and heartlessly.*[1]

Mike Regele, church consultant

### Active Vision, Not Wandering Aimlessness

The mainline churches have, all of them, stumbled and staggered their way into the twenty-first century—it has not been a pretty sight. Grand plans are occasionally hatched within their midst, and sweeping and high-sounding statements are issued with monotonous regularity, but when the rubber hits the road, most of them—both denominations and congregations—do not seem to have much clue of where they are headed, what their primary task should be, or why it is that conservative and evangelical congregations, denominational and nondenominational, blossom while much that has been at the heart of their lives continues to wither.

These words may sound harsh, sweeping, and dismissive, when compared to the smooth tones of established leadership that tells us either that there is no crisis or that in the long-term we really do not have too much to worry about. These may not be words that Episcopalians and other mainliners want to hear, but the truth is that even if the emperor is not entirely naked, he has very few clothes left on—which means that the same-old, same-old is just not going to hack it as we enter this strange new world that is being born. Meanwhile, the pace of change is heating up, and it behooves us to be responsive to the missionary challenge that today's culture offers us, instead of wasting time, energy, and resources on the constant bloodletting that has become the trademark of the older churches in the last two generations. It would seem that reaction, counterreaction, and an endless succession of splits and self-inflicted wounds has become our *modus vivendi*.

The 1990s were a tough decade for the historical churches of America, and although it has been with us for only a short time, so far the twenty-first century is not off to a particularly rosy start. Methodist leader Tom Oden says that he sees a slow shift toward positive changes in his church, and some of the signs are there in other churches, but we have a very long way to go before we get back to anything approaching theological, spiritual, and missional health.[2] As I look at all the fighting and squabbling that mars the face of the churches, I sometimes wonder if we are not like a handful of individuals afloat on an inflatable life raft in midocean. So determined are we that those whom we consider our opponents will not survive that we are all busy punching holes in the vessel—oblivious to the fact that we will very likely destroy our own lives in the process.

The time has come for us to attempt to move beyond our bitter feuding and find ways to uphold both truth and unity. Perhaps we need to create firewalls to insulate ourselves from those with whom we cannot agree, so that we can get on with the real work of the church—taking the news of God's Kingdom into the world for which God's Son died and rose again. Although having said that, on bad days I fear that in the Episcopal Church, at least, it might already be too late. This is a time when the fields are ripe for harvesting, but many of us seem to have lost the vision for sharing God's grace with a needy world.

### The Purpose of Trends

When Roger White and I wrote *New Millennium, New Church* a decade ago, the book was rather a novel approach to looking at the challenges before the church, so it tended to be treated by many as light Episcopal entertainment: "Let's bring on Kew and White and see what strange things they have to tell us!" This was not our intention, although we are glad so many people bought the book and enjoyed reading it. Looking back at what we wrote just a decade ago, the church seems to have been a gentler, more innocent (and far less complex) entity. The trends that we identified were encouraging—and a good number of the things that we anticipated might happen have come to pass. The book helped people deal with the challenge that the 1990s seemed to be offering.

This present book is meant to help readers deal with a whole new set of challenges that the 2000s are offering us. For those who can catch the vision of what God might do in the months and years ahead, the trends that have been pointed up here are signposts to direct us, help us shape our strategies, and focus our discipleship. They tell us something of the opportunities, and the difficulties, that might lie ahead of us. With each passing day we are moving into choppier waters, as far as the prevailing culture is concerned, so we ignore the signs of the times at our own peril.

Trends are not so much fixed points around which everything has to revolve, but markers that enable us to understand and interpret the topography. They help us survey what might lie ahead so that we can dream dreams, cast visions, and plan accordingly. It was always told to me in my youth by various of my teachers in high school, university, and seminary, that to be forewarned is to be forearmed, and that is precisely what a set of trends is—an opportunity to forearm ourselves for what might lie around the corner. But remember, even those of us who identify the various trends shaping the culture may get things badly wrong, because we are unable to see all the possible trajectories that history may take. We are, in a way, like weather forecasters whose computer model is always going to be inadequate when set alongside the realities.

It was secular futurist John L. Petersen who introduced me to the notion of wild cards. These are revolutionary and unexpected events or developments that will inevitably occur from time to time. "Wild cards have a low probability of occurrence but a very high impact, if they do."[3] There are all sorts of wild cards that can send the trends shooting off in any number of unexpected directions, just as an unexpected conjunction of weather fronts can suddenly upset predictions and send picnickers running for cover.

My good friend and leading Christian futurist Tom Sine confesses that this is what happened to him in a previous book that he wrote. "I missed a major change when I wrote *Wild Hope*, published in the U.S. in 1991. I correctly projected the creation of three major economic coalitions in the Americas, Europe, and Asia. But I didn't anticipate the decline in the Japanese economy, even though I had a colleague—a businessman—who accurately predicted what would happen."

Sine goes on to draw an important conclusion from this. "In spite of the fact that we sometimes get it wrong in this business of attempting to make sense of the future, we have only two options. Either we can ignore change entirely and live our lives, raise our young, and run our organizations as if the future were simply going to be more of what's happening now . . . or we can make our best efforts to anticipate some of the change racing toward us, so we have lead time to respond to it."[4]

What is important is that we learn to use our God-given intelligence and ability to observe what is going on so that we can, perhaps, identify here and there how God the Creator is at work within history. These various trends are an attempt to spell out what God might be doing in an orderly and systematic way. Just as sailing ships use rudder and sails to direct the winds and the currents to their destination, so we as Christians are enabled by God to use the winds and currents of time to move the cause of the Kingdom forward, rather than being tossed to and fro by the waves and furies.

### Developing a Way to Address the Future

The average congregation, it seems, would prefer to be a piece of flotsam and jetsam rather than have some understanding of its own potential for Christian service within the context of the flow of time. I have said countless times that many of the parishes that I visit seem to plan from Sunday bulletin to Sunday bulletin, with the annual budget providing outer limits of long-range strategizing. The mindset in too many congregations is "If only we can get to the end of another year, then we will survive." Just trying to survive is no longer good enough in today's bracing climate of change.

In the twenty-first century we need to shed our amateurish approach to strategizing and realize that our vocation as servants demands that we seek to see our way ahead and that we do our utmost for God's highest. For many, buffeted by the stresses and strains of daily existence, the life of the church actually becomes an escape, rather than the setting in which we attempt to make meaningful to the wider world the One who gives substance to life's realities and whose Cross is the center point of time and history. This means using the little gray cells with creativity and imagination so that we might be ministers of the grace that has been poured upon us from on high.

It is my dream that as parishes think, dream, and pray, they will develop teams of Christians whose skills and insights enable them to peer into the future and see what wonderful things God might do in their midst if they were but prepared for it. Just once or twice in the last twenty-five to thirty years I have found myself surrounded by Christians who so want to serve the Lord who died for them that they have sought to marry intelligent research with prayer and dreaming—the result has always been a breathtaking vision and extraordinary outcomes. To function in this way requires both courage and creativity, but it also needs a large dose of audacity.

There are resources out there to help organizations as they seek to turn raw dreams into meaningful visions for serving God in a whole succession of tomorrows. I highly recommend both the books and the services of Tom and Christine Sine, Christian futures consultants through their organization Mustard Seed Associates, and Episcopal Christians who have a great love for and commitment to the future mission of the mainline churches. Tom Sine's book *Mustard Seed Versus McWorld* contains one of the best summaries of all the futures tools available to us of which I know. People like the Sines, thoughtful and skilled futures-thinkers, are there to be used by churches, judicatories, and church institutions as we develop our future.[5] And, of course, I would be negligent if I did not admit to doing some of these things myself.

It is my contention that ministry in the new millennium is going to be more demanding than it has ever been. The challenges before us are gargantuan—there is an overwhelming number of pitfalls for the faith looming open before us like a gaping cavern, but for creative Christians the payback could be incredible. While there is a sufficiency about God's grace as we seek to serve him, it has never been easy to be wholehearted Christian disciples—and the coming century is going to be no exception. Yet the Good News in Jesus Christ has extraordinary power to redeem and transform, giving sight to the blind and setting the captive free.

It is also my contention that, if we can make ourselves available to God for forthright service, then the twenty-first century, which we enter in a high measure of disarray, could turn out to be the greatest missionary century in the history of the Christian faith. While God is the one who enables, this will happen only if we now put our hands to the plough, learn to dream God's dreams, and then to follow in his wake. One of the things that I have learned about futuring is that if it does not go hand-in-hand with praying it is little more than idle speculation. As we look at the future, whether we are optimists, pessimists, or somewhere in between, it is only by praying that we will learn the mind of God. Thus, all planning and dreaming needs to be undertaken with the Cross before us, and ourselves on our knees at its base.

I got up at 3:30 a.m. Central Standard Time on Friday, December 31, 1999, in order to watch the arrival of the New Year in each of the time zones around the world. It was something I felt that I had to do—and the television was on for most of the day, with me slumped in my recliner in front of it. I loved the spirited dancing of those Polynesian islanders who saw in the new century on the shores of a tiny dot of land in the Pacific that is closest to the International Date Line. I enjoyed the fireworks from Auckland—getting a much better view of what was going on than did a friend whose house has a glorious view overlooking the New Zealand city's picturesque harbor. Then we moved on to Sydney, Moscow, and other places that I have visited over the years.

Like millions of others of British heritage who understand the protocols about touching the monarch, I laughed and cried as Prince Philip and Prime Minister Tony Blair grabbed the hands of the startled Queen in the Millennium Dome in London for the traditional singing of "Auld Lang Sine." Truly, as the calendar rolled forward into 2000, old-fashioned things like protocol in the presence of royalty could be laid aside for a few minutes.

Then there was a lull as the torch of time passed over the tiny mid-Atlantic communities like Greenland, before finally crossing the Atlantic Ocean to the new world. First in Newfoundland, then the rest of the Maritime Provinces, and then the Eastern Time Zone, the year 2000 was welcomed—mercifully, without the Y2K computer nightmare that many had forecast. After watching this, living as we did in the Central Time Zone, our family headed for the church, where, with a surprising number of other members of our congregation, we greeted the new century silent and on our knees before the Almighty God, the ruler of time and space.

The arrival of 2000 was something about which I had dreamed and fantasized for a long time, yet when the moment came as we knelt in prayer in the silence of the sanctuary, all the hoopla seemed somewhat anticlimactic. The turning of a century is something of a symbol, however, of the extraordinary changes that are sweeping our world. Jesus, who is the same, yesterday, today, and forever, accompanies us as we make this journey into the future—so let us move ahead with him assured that we are not alone as we seek to serve him in the age that is emerging.

> A book like this is not meant to be the final word on a subject, but is meant to stimulate questions, ideas, and conversation. Part of my Web site, www.TheKewFiles.net, is set up to enable you to do just that. So, please, come along and visit, and discover how you can be part of the follow-through.

# NOTES

### INTRODUCTION
*Trends Come ... And Trends Go*

1.  John Naisbitt and Patricia Aburdene, *Megatrends 2000* (New York: William Morrow & Co., 1990).
2.  Richard Kew and Roger White, *New Millennium, New Church* (Boston: Cowley Publications, 1992).
3.  The trends that we identified for the Episcopal Church in *New Millennium, New Church* were: 1. The Renewal Movements Come of Age. 2. The Liberal Consensus Begins to Erode. 3. A Groundswell toward Creedal Orthodoxy. 4. The Mushrooming of Spirituality and Formation Movements. 5. The Liturgical Revolution Comes to an End. 6. The Rising Profile of Women. 7. New Ministers for a New Millennium. 8. Outsiders Flock to the Episcopal Church. 9. A New Confidence in Evangelism. 10. The Continued Priority of Stewardship. 11. The Spread of Single-Issue Organizations. 12. The Rise of Networks, the Decline of Hierarchy. 13. Episcopalians as World Christians.
4.  William A. Sheridan, *The Fortune Sellers* (New York: John Wiley & Sons, 1998), p. 14.
5.  If you want a brief guide at how to do this, then the second chapter of *Mustard Seed Versus McWorld* by Tom Sine could help you.

### TREND ONE
*Globalization Will Continue Apace*

1.  Thomas L. Friedman, *The Lexus and the Olive Tree* (New York: Farrar, Straus, Giroux, 1999).

2. I am grateful to my South African friend Graeme Codrington, for reminding me of this fact.
3. For more information about this you can read *Globalization and History: The Evolution of a Nineteenth-Century Economy* by Kevin O'Rourke and Jeffrey Williamson (Cambridge, MA: MIT Press, 1999).
4. John Micklethwait and Adrian Wooldridge, *A Future Perfect* (New York: Crown Business, 2000), p. ix.
5. These range from what might happen if Russia were to totally unravel, to the possibility of nuclear hostilities between India and Pakistan.
6. There is an excellent article about this region by Simon Winchester in the January 2000 issue of *National Geographic Magazine.*
7. *The Economist,* January 22, 2000, *A Tale of Two Debtors,* p. 17.
8. William Strauss and Neil Howe, *Generations: The History of America's Future, 1584 to 2069* (New York, William Morrow and Company, 1991), and *The Fourth Turning* (New York: Broadway Books, 1996)
9. *The Fourth Turning,* 272–73.
10. Neil Howe & William Strauss, *Millennials Rising: The Next Great Generation* (New York: Vintage Press, 2000), p. 16.
11. Quoted from a private e-mail from Graeme Codrington, a South African youth minister and youth ministry specialist.
12. *A Future Perfect,* xx.
13. Ibid., p. 197.
14. Tom Sine, *Mustard Seed Versus McWorld* (Grand Rapids, MI: Baker Book House, 1999).
15. You can join the Toward2015 online discussion by logging onto http://listserv.episcopalian.org and following the instructions.
16. Quoted from a personal e-mail.
17. Anglican Frontier Missions, advised by the Reverend Dr. David B. Barrett, Anglican priest and researcher, has been one of the pioneers in using today's communications technology to spread the Gospel and reach the least evangelized. If you want to know about AFM and their non-residential missionary program, you can contact their executive director, the Reverend E. A. de Bordenave, at afmxc.org, or at their Web site at www.episcopalian.org. Similar work is being undertaken in other denominations and by a variety of nondenominational organizations.
18. Archbishop Marcello Zago of the Vatican, *Missiology,* XXVIII, No. 1 (January 2000), p. 7.

19. Andrew Walls, *The Missionary Movement in Christian History* (Maryknoll, NY: Orbis Books, 1996), p. xiii. Following missionary service in Sierra Leone, Professor Walls was on the faculties of the Universities of Aberdeen and then Edinburgh.
20. The Missionary Movement in Christian History, p. xiii

## TREND TWO
### *A Process of Radical Ecclesiastical Reconfiguration*

1. Loren B. Mead, *Once and Future Church* (Washington, D.C.: The Alban Institute, 1991), p. 16.
2. Phyllis Tickle, religion editor of *Publishers Weekly,* quoted in the Context newsletter of Martin Marty (January 15, 2000, 32, No. 2). Tickle goes on to point out one of the consequences of this. She say that "as hierarchies falter, the production of spiritual and religious materials, even curricular ones, will fall more and more to free-standing or non-church-affiliated houses."
3. Taken from an article published online in February 2000 by Virtuosity, the Internet news service of journalist David Virtue.
4. George W. Bullard in *Net Results.* (November-December 2000, p. 28).
5. St. Andrew's Church, Little Rock, Arkansas, a congregation that was established by a group of former members of Trinity Cathedral, Little Rock, was denied membership of the Diocese of Arkansas, and so was given a home as an extra-territorial congregation of a diocese of the church in Rwanda. Meanwhile, Christ Church, Grove Farm, Pennsylvania, is pastored by a Caucasian priest who continues to be a member of the Episcopal Diocese of Pittsburgh. His congregation, however, has full membership of a diocese of the Church of Uganda. This latter case was with the blessing of the diocesan bishop of Pittsburgh. In addition to this, there is a small but growing number of Episcopal or former Episcopal congregations that work cooperatively with one another, but are affiliated with no part of the Communion.
6. On January 29, 2000, John Rodgers and Charles H. Murphy, III, were consecrated to the episcopate to serve as missionary bishops of the churches of Singapore and Rwanda, but working in the U.S.A. by Abp. Moses Tay of Southeast Asia, Abp. Emmanuel Kolini of Rwanda, and Bp. John Rucyana of the Rwandan Church. Also participating were C. FitzSimons Allison, Retired Bishop of South

Carolina, and Alex Dickson, Retired Bishop of West Tennessee. Their consecration appears to have been the first step in the establishment of a parallel and more conservative province now known as the Anglican Mission in America (AMiA).

7.  This is quoted from a letter that Bishop Charles H. Murphy, III, sent to the First Promise movement in the Episcopal Church in August 2000.

8.  During 2000, both the Evangelical Lutheran Church of America and the Episcopal Church of the U.S.A. agreed to the "Call to Common Mission," a plan that will go a long way toward merging the mission and ministry of the two denominations.

9.  William Willimon in an article called "To the Church Called Mainline," in *Christianity Today*, (October 25, 1999, www.christianityonline.come/ct/9TC/9TC069.html).

10. Leonard Sweet, *SoulTsunami* (Grand Rapids, MI: Zondervan Publishing House, 1999), p. 19.

11. William Strauss and Neil Howe, *Generations—The History of America's Future, 1584 to 2069* (New York: William Morrow and Company, 1991), p. 320.

12. Leonard Sweet, *Aqua Church* (Loveland, Colorado: Group Publishing, 1999), p. 28. *Silents and G.I.'s Still Control the Machinery.*

13. Robert E. Webber, *Ancient-Future Faith* (Grand Rapids, MI: Baker Book House, 1999), p. 27.

14. In 1997, in his book *Tattered Trust* (Nashville, TN: Abingdon Press), Lyle E. Schaller, the dean of church consultants, urged the mainline churches to think seriously about moving away from geographical judicatories to ones where ethnicity, theological bias, or the like, provide the commonalities. This, he asserted, was the only way for unity of any kind to be maintained.

15. William Willimon in an article called *To the Church Called Mainline*, in *Christianity Today*, October 25, 1999.

TREND THREE
*The Future Lies with Mission-Driven Units*

1.  Alister McGrath, *The Renewal of Anglicanism* (Harrisburg, PA: Morehouse Publishing, 1993), p. 24.

2.  The Alpha Course was developed at Holy Trinity Church, Brompton, London, and has since the mid-nineties spread around the world. It is said in England that today no one is beyond walking distance of an Alpha Course. Alpha is an unthreatening, hos-

pitality-rich approach to giving the unchurched a chance to ask questions of Christians, while at the same time discovering what the faith is *really* all about. Emmaus is a comprehensive study program for churches, designed to welcome newcomers as they take their first steps on a lifelong journey into faith. Through Emmaus people are invited to faith, then nurtured to grow into mature disciples.

3. From the address of the Bishop of Albany at the 1999 Diocesan Convention (www.albanyepiscopaldiocese.org).
4. *The Renewal of Anglicanism,* p. 6.
5. If you would like to learn more about MimosaNet, the name of our forward-looking leaders' network, please e-mail either Kevin Martin (canonkevin@worldnet.att.net) or me (RichardKew@aol.com). In due course, we expect to have a Web site up and running, although this is at the moment very much an informal group of dreamers and practitioners.
6. Researchers have visited certain parts of the country and have counted the cars outside churches during Sunday worship. The estimated attendance on the basis of the parking lot census do not match the claims for church attendance that are being made.
7. *SoulTsunami,* p. 50.
8. Wilbert R. Shenk, *Write the Vision—The Church Renewed* (Valley Forge, PA: Trinity Press International, 1995), p. 54.
9. I have had the good fortune and privilege to be appointed to the task force that will work with Challenge.
10. Quoted by Christine D. Pohl in *Making Room: Recovering Hospitality as a Christian Tradition* (Grand Rapids, MI: Wm. B. Eerdman Publishing Co., 1999), p. 6.
11. Christine Pohl, *Making Room: Recovering Hospitality as a Christian Tradition* (Grand Rapids, MI: Wm. Eerdmans Publishing Co., 1999) pp. 3, 8, 10.
12. *The New York Times,* July 2, 2000.
13. C. Peter Wagner, *The Healthy Church* (Ventura, CA: Regal Books, 1996), p. 23.

TREND FOUR
*A Growing Mound of Major Fiscal Challenges*

1. Ronald J. Sider, *Rich Christians in an Age of Hunger: A Biblical Study* (Downers Grove, IL: InterVarsity Press, 1977), pp. 172–173.

2. In the summer of 2000, the Anglican Church of Canada found it necessary to significantly reduce personnel and program in order to balance books that were deeply in the red.
3. Sir John Templeton was one of the first American financiers to bet on the future of the Japanese economy during the 1950s, invested there quite heavily, and encouraged others to do so.
4. Peter Schwartz, quoted by Tom Sine in *Mustard Seed Versus Mc-World*, (Grand Rapids, MI: Baker Book House, 1999), p. 53.
5. Os Guiness (Ed.), *Unriddling Our Times* (Grand Rapids, MI: Baker Book House, 1999), p. 11.
6. *Mustard Seed*, p. 56.
7. Robert Wuthnow, *The Crisis in the Churches* (New York: Oxford University Press, 1997), p. 11.
8. *The Crisis in the Churches,* pp. 225–225.
9. This is by no means a fanciful notion. On February 22, 2000, the People's Republic of China made threats to attack Taiwan if the Taiwanese did not come to the negotiating table and begin the process of restoring its political links with the Chinese mainland.
10. Ronald E. Vallet and Charles E. Zech, *The Mainline Church's Funding Crisis: Issues and Possibilities* (Grand Rapids, MI; Manlius, NY: Wm. B. Eerdmans Publishing Co., and REV/Rose Publishing, 1995), p. 68.
11. Lyle E. Schaller, *Innovations in Ministry: Models for the Twenty-First Century* (Nashville, TN: Abingdon Press, 1994), p. 149.
12. One of the great anxieties of African Christians is the manner in which huge sums of money coming from the oil-rich Arab world are being used to advance the cause of Islam on their continent. The manner in which this money is used very often troubles them.

TREND FIVE
*Radically Changing Demographics*

1. Norman Shawchuck and Gustave Rath, *Benchmarks of Quality in the Church* (Nashville, TN: Abingdon Press, 1994), p. 12.
2. This is spelled out on p. 37.
3. Reported in "Canadian Churches Face Problem That Endangers Their Future," published in *Religion Watch*, Vol. 15, Number 3, January 2000.
4. The Zacchaeus Report was produced as a gift to the church by the

Episcopal Church Foundation in 1999, the fiftieth anniversary of the Foundation's life. It can be accessed from the Episcopal Church's Web site at www.dfms.org.

5. From a *Christianity Today* interview on August 11, 1997, entitled *The Spirit Hasn't Left the Mainline* (http://www.christianityon-line.com/ct/7T9/7T914b.html).

6. Younger clergy are also looking at the conundrum Commissions on Ministry create. Their "Gathering of the NeXt Generation" has developed a pilot project that they are calling the Young Priest Initiative to challenge CoM preconceptions.

7. From "The Evolution of Generation X Ministry," *Regeneration Quarterly* (Fall 1999, Vol. 5, Number 3).

8. Richard G. Hutchinson, *Mainline Churches and the Evangelicals— A Challenging Crisis?* (Atlanta, GA: John Knox Press, 1981), pp. 58–59.

9. Associated Press story of January 13, 2000, published by *The New York Times* online.

## TREND SIX
### The Fast Approaching Gray Wave

1. Robert D. Kaplan, *An American Wilderness* (New York: Random House, 1998), p. 18.

2. Marc Freedman, *Prime Time: How Baby Boomers Will Revolutionize Retirement and Transform America* (New York: Public Affairs, 1999), pp. 12–13.

3. Tom Sine argues his case most cogently in his book *Mustard Seed Versus McWorld* (Grand Rapids, MI: Baker Book House, 1999).

4. William Knoke, *Bold New World* (New York: Kodansha America, 1996), p. 64.

5. *Prime Time*, p. 224.

6. If you are interested in online Christian education and theological training, get in touch with www.online.tesm.edu, 311 Eleventh Street, Ambridge, PA 15003.

7. D. Larry Gregg, quoted in *Context*, March, 1, 2000.

8. St. Luke 2:21–40.

9. The following was reported in *The Washington Times* in January 2000: Jane Fonda has become a born-again Christian, enthusiastic in her newly found faith, and her conversion is making waves from Atlanta to Hollywood. She's regularly attending church services and Bible studies in Atlanta, and one friend calls her faith "very real,

very deep." News of her conversion—one of her longtime critics calls it a conversion "right up there with Saul of Tarsus"—leaped from Internet gossip to mainstream newspapers following the disclosure last week that she and her husband, Ted Turner, have separated. She had said in an interview two years ago, on the eve of her sixtieth birthday, that she had asked herself, "Where do I want to go with the last third of my life?"

TREND SEVEN
*An Array of Impossible Moral Dilemmas*

1. John L. Petersen, *The Road to 2015* (Corte Madera, CA: Waite Group Press, 1994), p. 69.
2. James Davidson Hunter, *Culture Wars* (New York: Harper and Row, 1991).
3. Peter Kreeft, *Ecumenical Jihad* (San Francisco: Ignatius Press, 1996), pp. 6, 39.
4. Eric Drexler quoted by John L. Petersen in *The Road to 2015,* p. 58.
5. Bill Joy explores at length the threat to human life as we know it from machines that are more intelligent than ourselves in an article in *Wired* magazine, "Why the Future Doesn't Need Us" (April 2000, pp. 238–262).
6. Announcement of this achievement was made on June 26, 2000, in Washington, D.C., by President Bill Clinton, and in London by Prime Minister Tony Blair.
7. "The Human Genome Is Mapped. Now What?" *Time* magazine online, July 3, 2000. (See www.time.com.)
8. *Newsweek,* "Decoding the Human Body." April 10, 2000.
9. Stanley Hauerwas in *What Would Pope Stanley Say?* (An interview with Rodney Clapp in *Books and Culture*, a CT Publication, November-December 1998).
10. From a timeline projected by Arthur C. Clarke in his book *Greetings, Carbon-Based Bipeds! Collected Essays 1934–1998* (New York: St. Martin's Press, 1999), and reported in *The Futurist* (March-April 2000).
11. Scott B. Rae and Paul M. Cox, *Bioethics: A Christian Approach in a Pluralistic Age* (Grand Rapids, MI: Wm. B. Eerdmans Publishing Co., 1999) pp. 112–14.
12. Lesslie Newbigin, *The Gospel in a Pluralist Society* (London: SPCK, 1989), p. 210. This is, in effect, a commentary by Newbigin on Ephesians 6:12ff.

13. "Why the Future Doesn't Need Us," from *Wired*. P. 243.

*The Continuing Spirituality Boom*

1.  John Drane, *Faith in a Changing Culture* (London: Marshall Pickering, 1997), p. 39.
2.  Marcus Borg and N. T. Wright, *The Meaning of Jesus—Two Visions* (San Francisco: HarperSanFrancisco, 1999), p. 158.
3.  George Gallup, Jr., and Timothy R. Jones, *The Next American Spirituality* (Colorado Springs: Cook Communications, 2000), p. 14.
4.  Faith Popcorn, *Clicking* (New York: HarperCollins, 1996), p. 126.
5.  Patrick Glynn, *God—The Evidence* (Rocklin, CA: Prima/Forum, 1997), p. 2.
6.  One of the people who has helped me with this book wrote to me the following: "In the small, blue-collar town where I serve, our church always has a bake sale at the town homecoming. I was sitting at the table with an elderly lifelong parishioner when a woman in Islamic dress passed by. In response to my parishioner's alarmed, whispered question about who that might be, I casually replied that I assumed she was a Muslim. My parishioner's eyes widened and she said, "Well, I didn't know they were allowed to be Muslims in America."
7.  *The Next American Spirituality*, p. 29.
8.  *Faith in a Changing Culture*, p. 16.
9.  *The Next American Spirituality*, p. 27.
10. Eugene H. Peterson, *Subversive Spirituality* (Grand Rapids, MI: Wm. B. Eerdmans Publishing Co., 1994, 1997), p. 38.
11. Stanley J. Grenz, *A Primer of Postmodernism* (Grand Rapids, MI: Wm. B. Eerdmans Publishing Co., 1996), p. 8.
12. Archbishop Marcello Zago, *The New Millennium and the Emerging Religious Encounters*, (*Missiology*, Vol. XXVIII, No. 1, January 2000).
13. *Ecumenical Jihad*. Peter Kreeft wrote at great length along these lines in his 1996 book.
14. Dallas Willard, *The Divine Conspiracy* (San Francisco: HarperSanFrancisco, 1998), pp. 41–42.
15. Context newsletter, January 15, 2000, Vol. 32, No. 2.
16. The leading British Catholic scholar, Aiden Nichols, O.P., commenting on contemporary liturgy says, "Liturgy is where Scripture, in a sense, comes most fully into its own, in the liturgical preaching and

in the way in which the liturgy is textured out of a myriad of biblical references. But it has to be Liturgy that is not so denatured so that it simply becomes an instrument of political correctness. Because in that case you're losing precisely its power to challenge and transform the way people are when they arrive. If the function of the Liturgy is simply to affirm people in their secular identities or those aspects of decent living that are available through secular agencies, then I don't see the Liturgy as having any special evangelical force. It must lift people up to something beyond their secular consciousness." Quoted from Conversation with Fr. Nichols, *Touchstone* magazine, November 2000, p. 30 (www.touchstonemag.com).

**TREND NINE**
*Learning to Live with and Love the Internet*

1. Nicholas Negroponte, *Being Digital* (London: Coronet/Hodder and Stoughton, 1995), p. 7.
2. *Being Digital*, p. 178.
3. When shopping online it is very important to check the credibility of an enterprise with whom you decide to do business—especially the security of their financial records and their ability to deliver what they promise.
4. Jeff Zalewski, *The Soul of Cyber Space* (San Francisco: Harper Edge, 1997), p. 4.
5. John Naisbitt, *Global Paradox* (New York: William Morrow and Co., 1994), pp. 23, 25.
6. Thomas L. Friedman, *The Lexus and the Olive Tree* (New York: Farrar, Straus Giroux, 1999), pp. 94–95.
7. This technology is discussed in Walter Kirn's article, "The Phone," in *The New York Times Magazine* (June 11, 2000, p. 90).
8. Stephen Bertman, *Hyperculture—The Human Cost of Speed* (Westpoint, Connecticut: Praeger, 1998), p. 96–97.
9. *Hyperculture*, p. 128.

**TREND TEN**
*Massive Theological Rethinking*

1. Robert E. Webber, *Ancient-Future Faith* (Grand Rapids, MI: Baker Book House, 1999), p. 14.
2. This was in the lead story of *Religion Watch* in February 2000 (Vol. 15, No. 4), "Evangelicals' Postmodern Identity Crisis?"

3. Graham Cray, *The Post-Evangelical Debate* (London: SPCK/Triangle Books, 1997), pp. 2–3.

4. Alan J. Roxburgh, *The Missionary Congregation, Leadership, and Liminality* (Harrisburg, PA: Trinity Press International, 1997), p. 45.

5. This was one of the theses explored by noted Scots missiologist, Andrew Walls, in a series of lectures he delivered at Trinity Episcopal School for Ministry, Ambridge, Pennsylvania, in October 1999.

6. Timothy Dudley-Smith, *John Stott: The Making of a Leader* (Downers Grove, IL: InterVarsity Press, 1999), p. 187.

7. McGrath makes this observation in his book *J.I. Parker: A Biography* (Grand Rapids, MI: Baker Book House, 1997), p. 212.

8. Leander Keck, *The Church Confident* (Nashville, TN: Abingdon Press, 1993), p. 45.

9. Thomas C. Oden, *Requiem—Lament in Three Movements* (Nashville, TN: Abingdon Press, 1995), p. 46.

10. John Shelby Spong, *Here I Stand—My Struggle for a Christianity of Integrity, Love, and Equality* (San Francisco: HarperSanFrancisco, 2000), p. 387.

11. This statement is quoted in "Mission, Renewal, and the Future of the Church," an article first published in the *International Bulletin of Missionary Research,* October 1997, Vol. 21, No. 4, p. 158.

12. Paul Lakeland, *Postmodernity—Christian Identity in a Fragmented Age* (Minneapolis: Fortress Press, 1997), pp. ix-x.

CONCLUSION
## Why Trends?

1. Mike Regele, *The Death of the Church* (Grand Rapids, MI: Zondervan, 1995), p. 234.

2. In an article entitled "Mainstreaming the Mainline," Oden discusses some of the positive things legislated at the United Methodist General Conference in May 2000 in Cleveland, Ohio. He sees these as hopeful signs in the long-term (*Christianity Today,* August 7, 2000, pp. 59–61).

3. John L. Petersen, *The Road to 2015* (Corte Madera: Waite Group Press, 1994), p. 288.

4. *Mustard Seed Versus McWorld*, p. 37.

5. The Sines can be reached at Mustard Seed Associates, 510 NE 81st Street, Seattle, WA 98115. Phone: 206–524-2111.